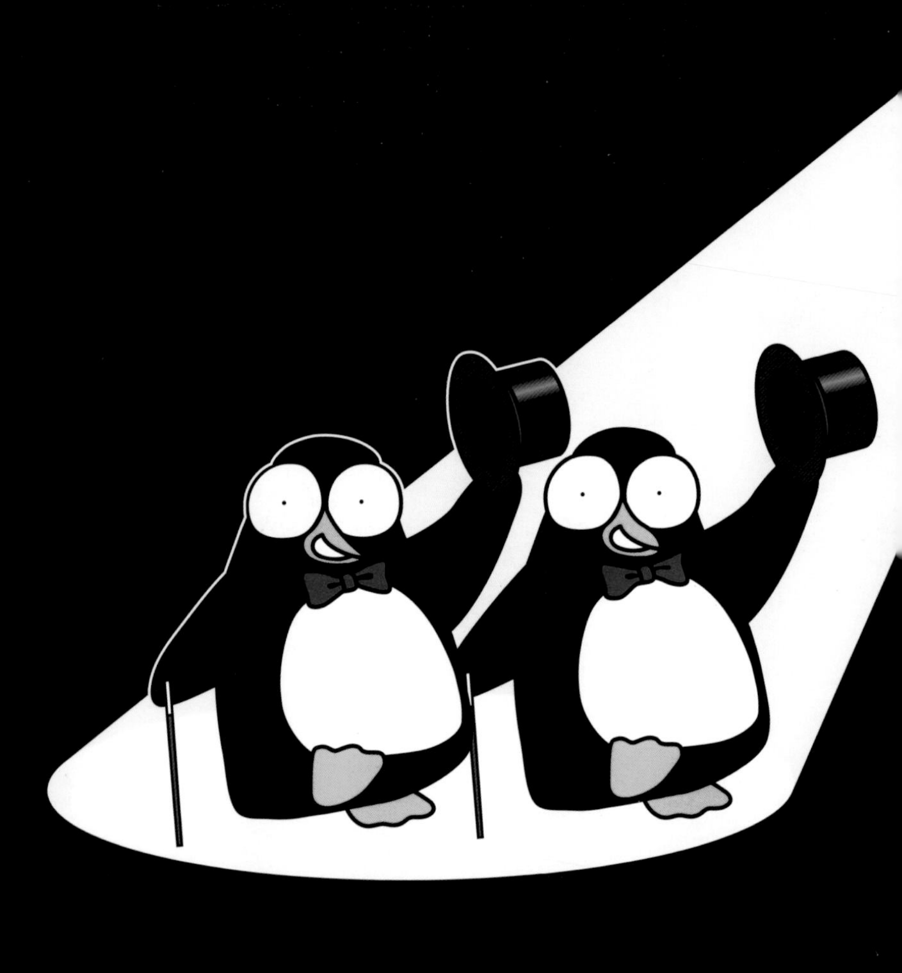

GUS & WALDO's
BOOK OF LOVE

by
Massimo Fenati

The right of Massimo Fenati to be identified as the author of this work has been asserted by him in accordance with the Copyright, Designs and Patents Act 1988.

First published in hardback in Great Britain in 2006 by Orion Books, an imprint of the Orion Publishing Group Ltd
Orion House, 5 Upper St Martin's Lane,
London WC2H 9EA

10 9 8 7 6 5 4 3 2 1

A CIP catalogue record for this book is available from the British Library.

ISBN-10: 0 75287 565 5
ISBN-13: 978 0 75287 565 1

Designed by Massimo Fenati
Printed in Italy by Printer Trento

Every effort has been made to fulfil requirements with regard to reproducing copyright material. The author and publisher will be glad to rectify any omissions at the earliest opportunity.

www.orionbooks.co.uk
www.gusandwaldo.com

The Orion Publishing Group's policy is to use papers that are natural, renewable and recyclable and made from wood grown in sustainable forests. The logging and manufacturing processes are expected to conform to the environmental regulations of the country of origin.

Thanks to:

Barbara Albericci, Lorna-Dawn Creanor,
Tess Cuming, Maria Dawson, Ian Dunkley,
Sam Edenborough, Claire Gill, Jelena Joksimovic,
Nicki Kennedy, Sophie Laurimore,
Alex Menzies, Emily Sklar, Martin Turner
and everybody at Orion.

And very special thanks to:

Amanda Harris, Simon Trewin,
Serena Brugnolo, Liza Enebeis
and Walter Iuzzolino.

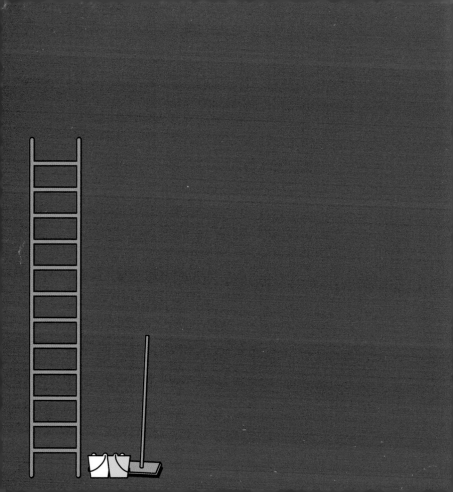

for Walter

Gus and Waldo

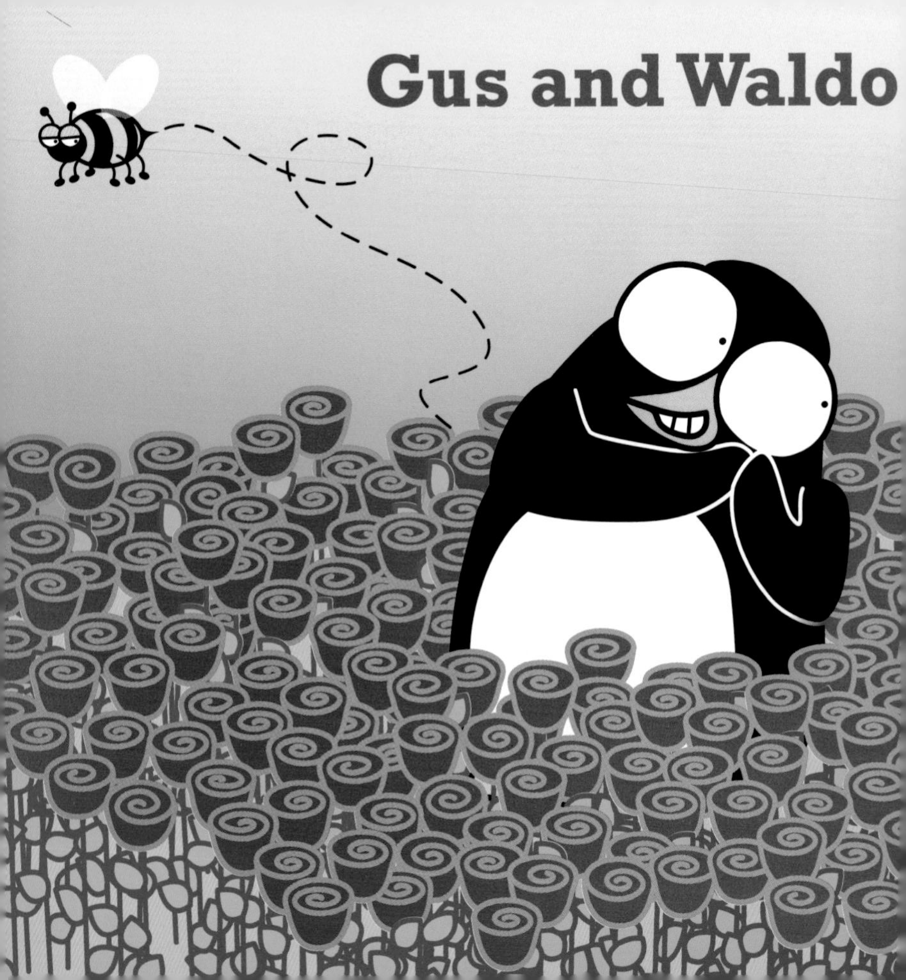

are in love

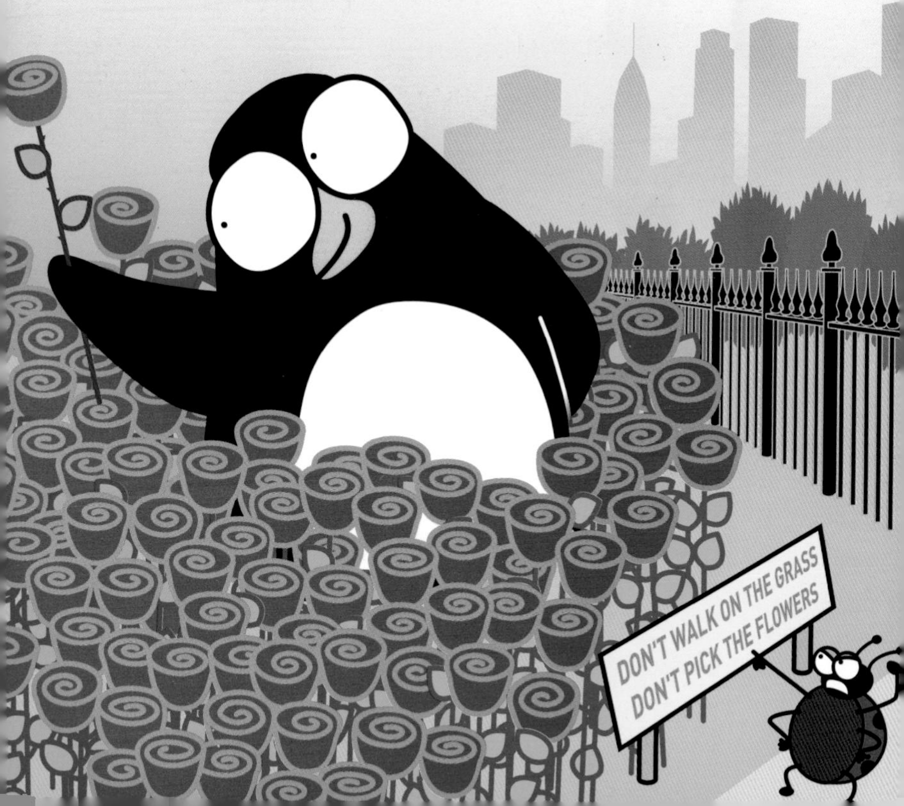
DON'T WALK ON THE GRASS
DON'T PICK THE FLOWERS

But once upon

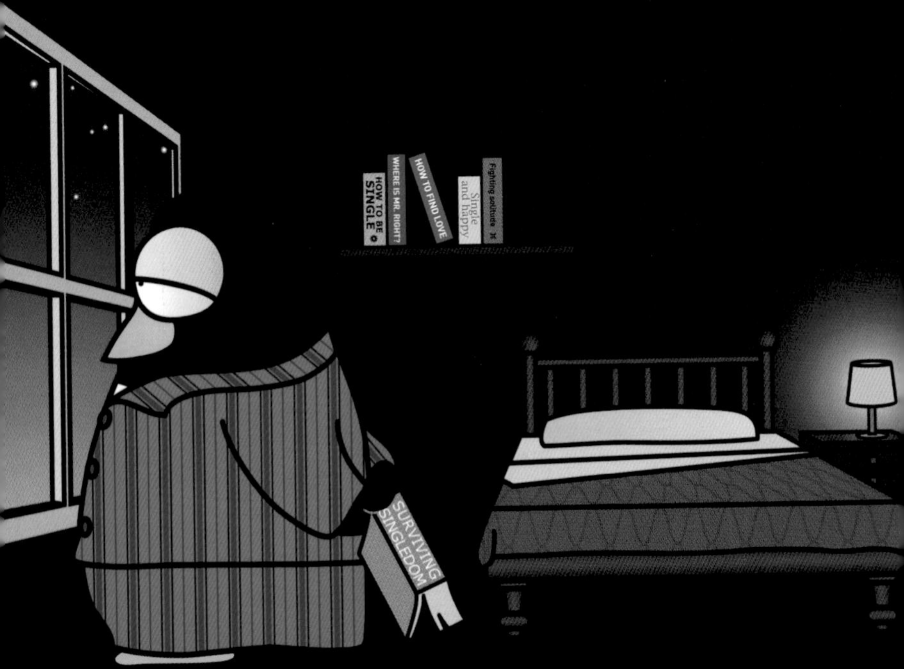
HOW TO BE SINGLE
WHERE IS MR. RIGHT?
HOW TO FIND LOVE
Single and happy
Fighting solitude
SURVIVING SINGLEDOM

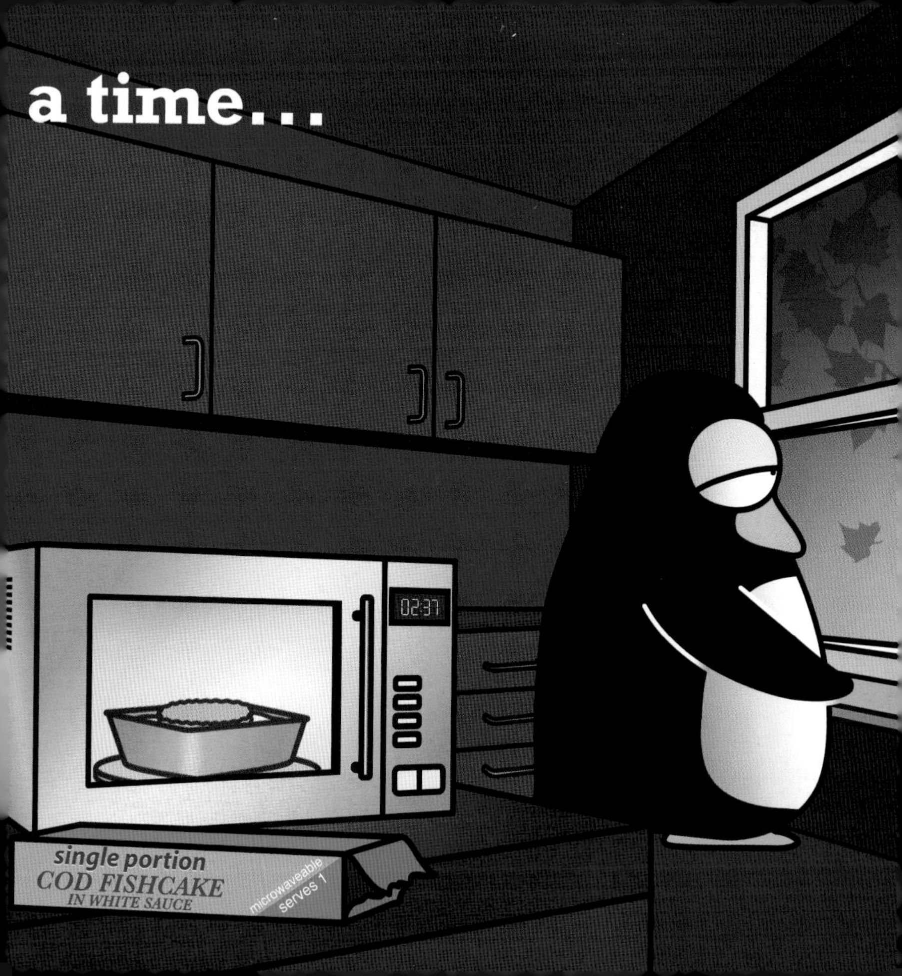
a time...
02:37
single portion
COD FISHCAKE
IN WHITE SAUCE
microwaveable
serves 1

...they were single...

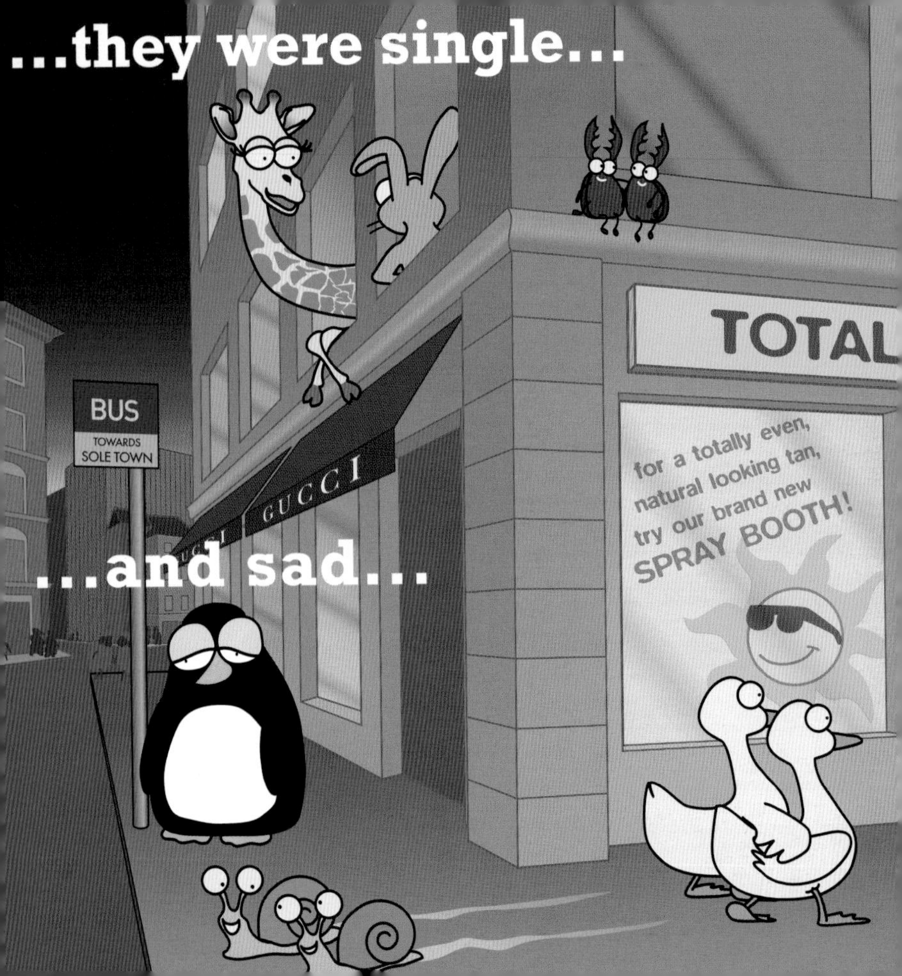
BUS
TOWARDS SOLE TOWN
GUCCI
GUCCI
TOTAL
for a totally even, natural looking tan, try our brand new SPRAY BOOTH!

...and sad...

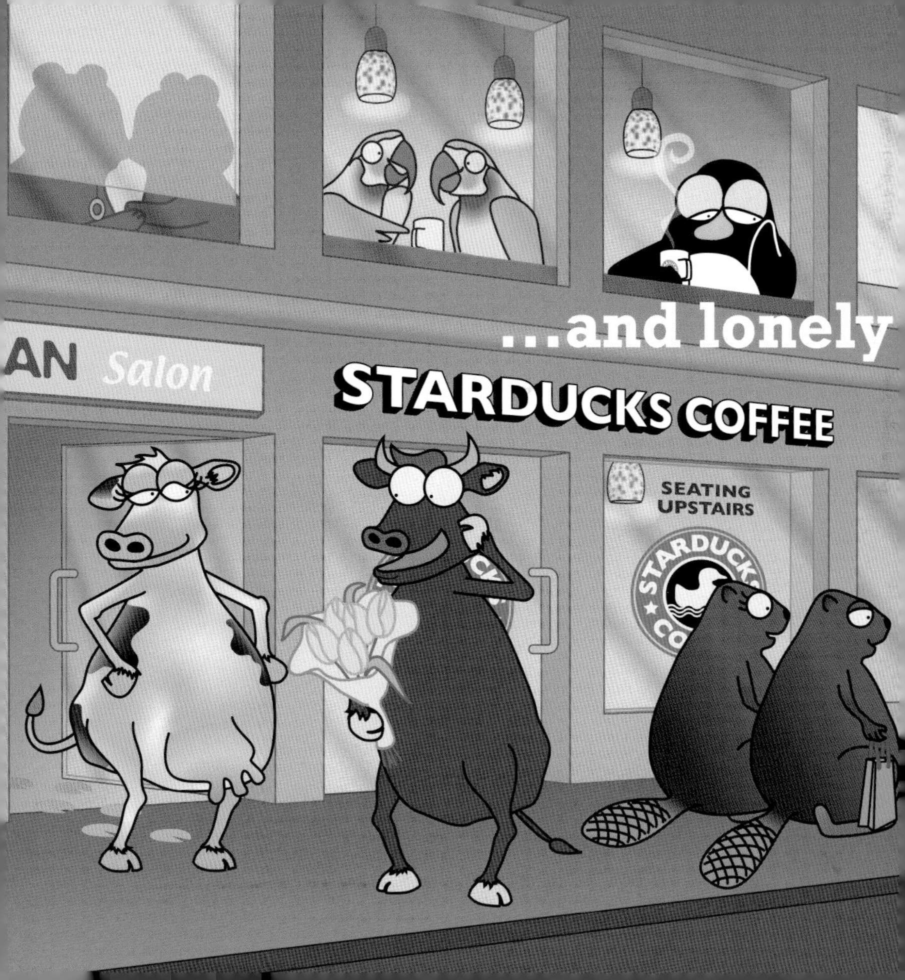
AN Salon
STARDUCKS COFFEE
SEATING UPSTAIRS
STARDUCKS

...and lonely

Nothing made

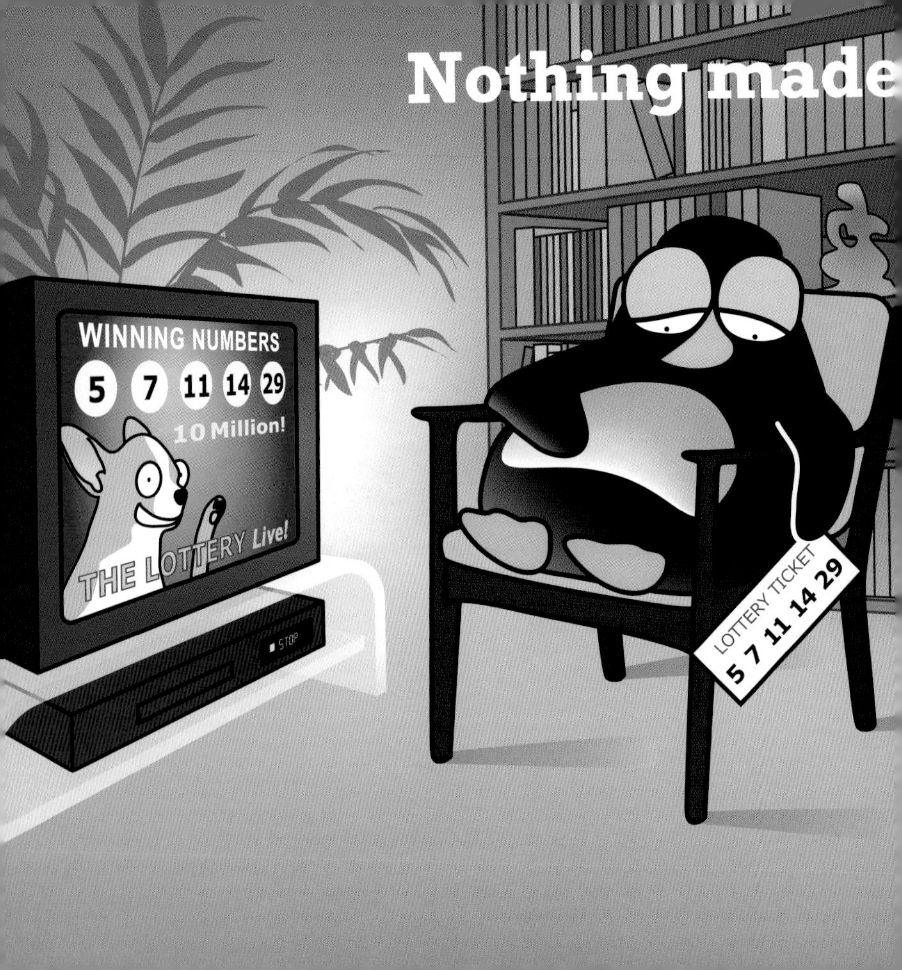
WINNING NUMBERS
5 7 11 14 29
10 Million!
THE LOTTERY Live!
STOP
LOTTERY TICKET
5 7 11 14 29

them happy

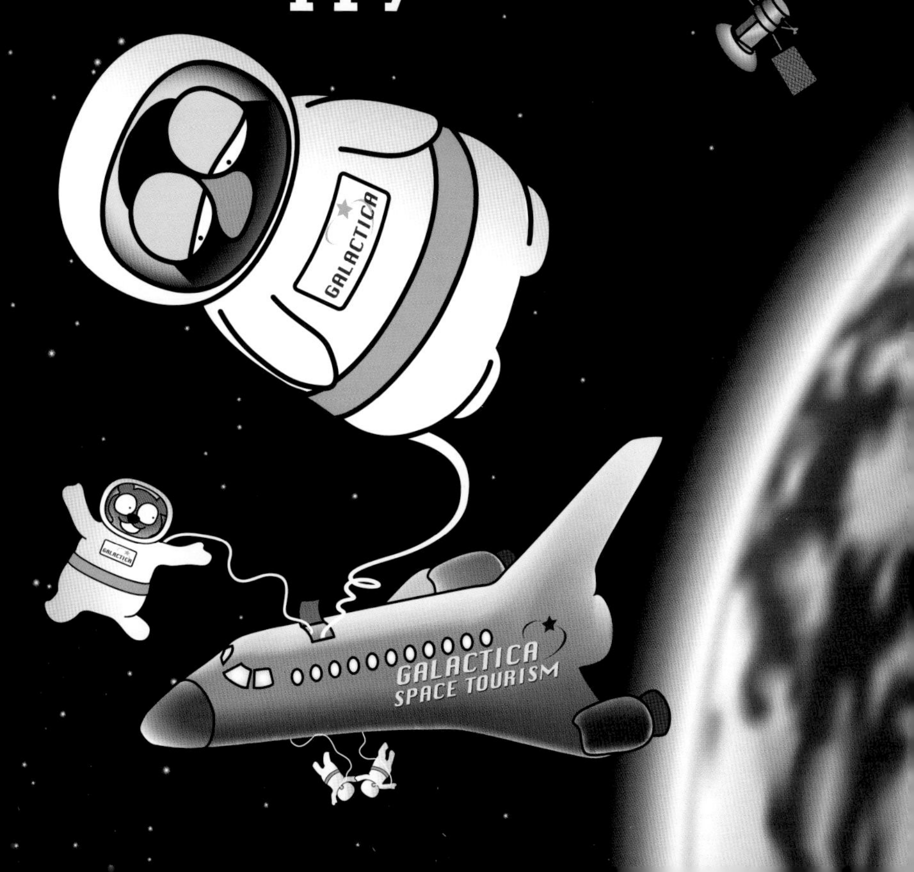
GALACTICA
GALACTICA
GALACTICA
SPACE TOURISM

Nothing made them smile

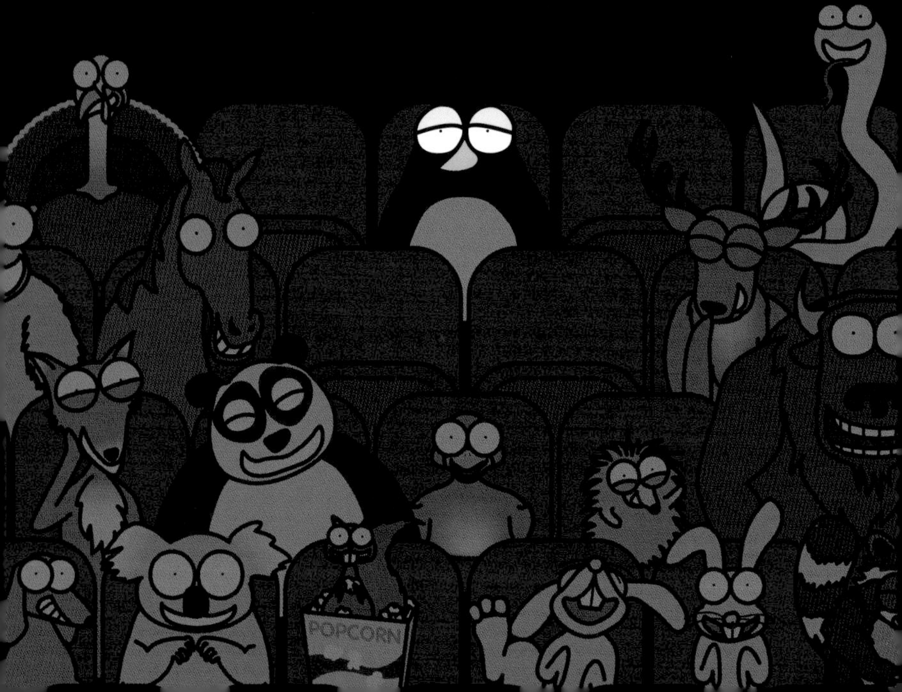
POPCORN

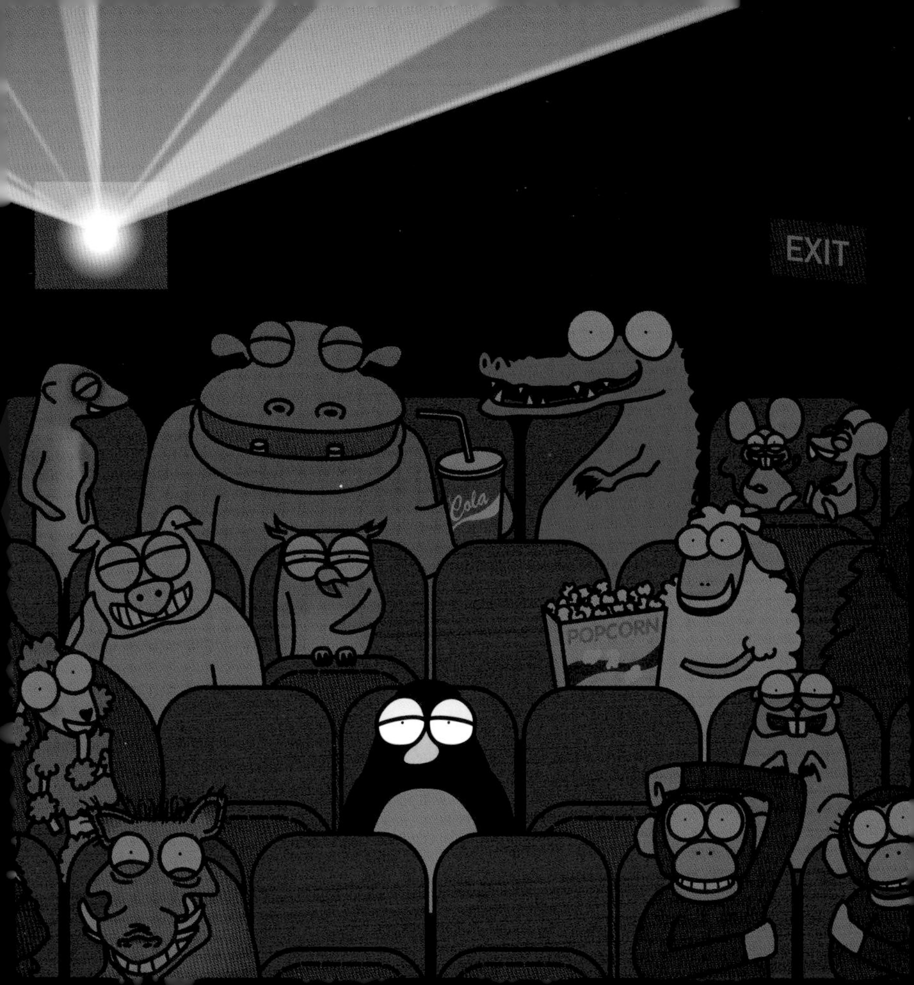
EXIT
Cola
POPCORN

But ther

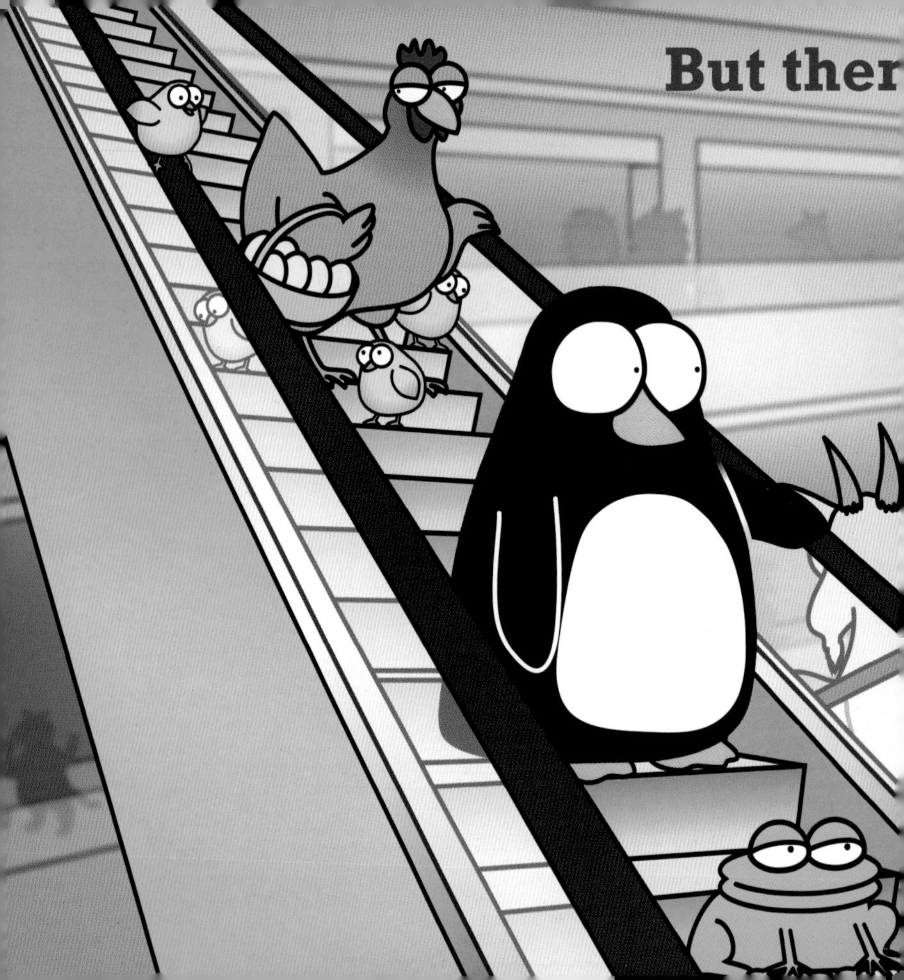

one day...

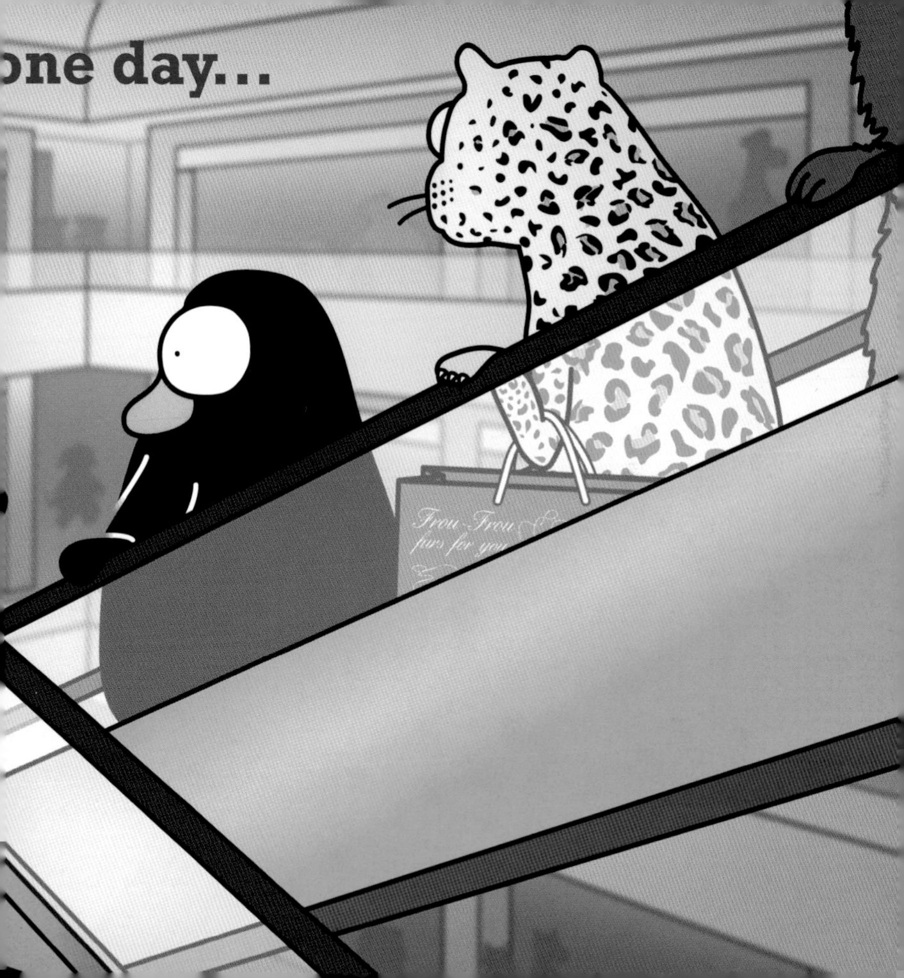
Frou-Frou
furs for you

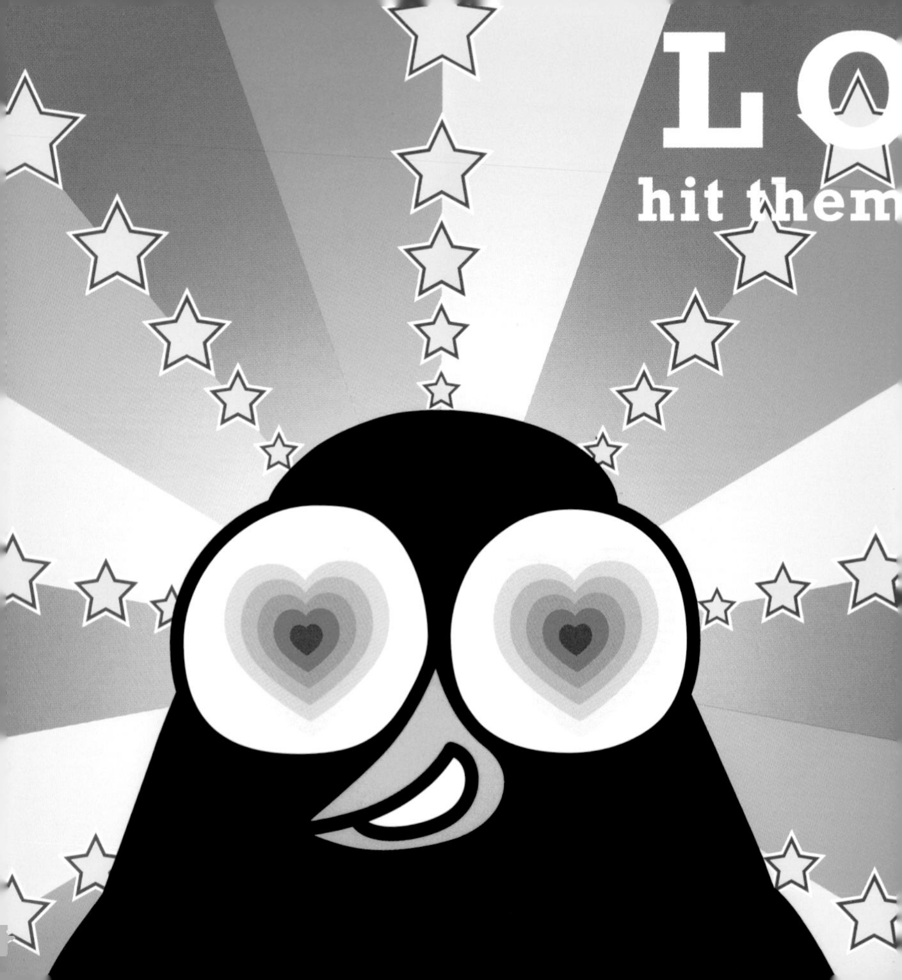
LO
hit them

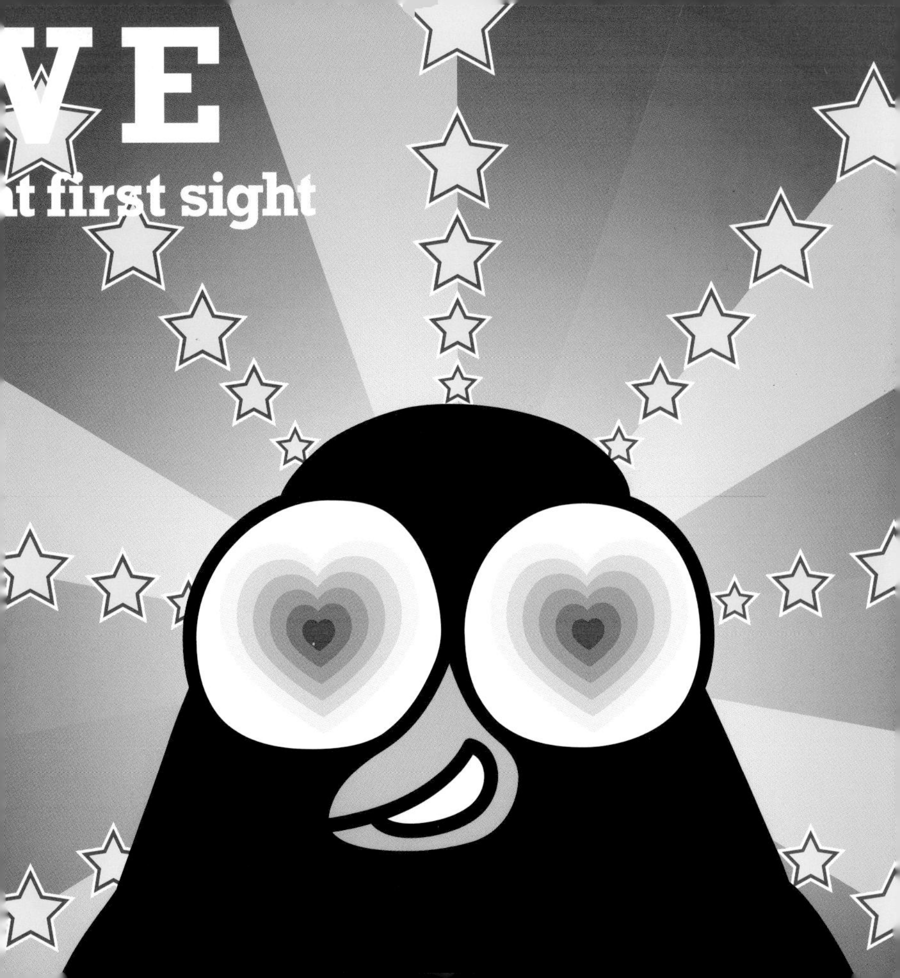
VE
t first sight

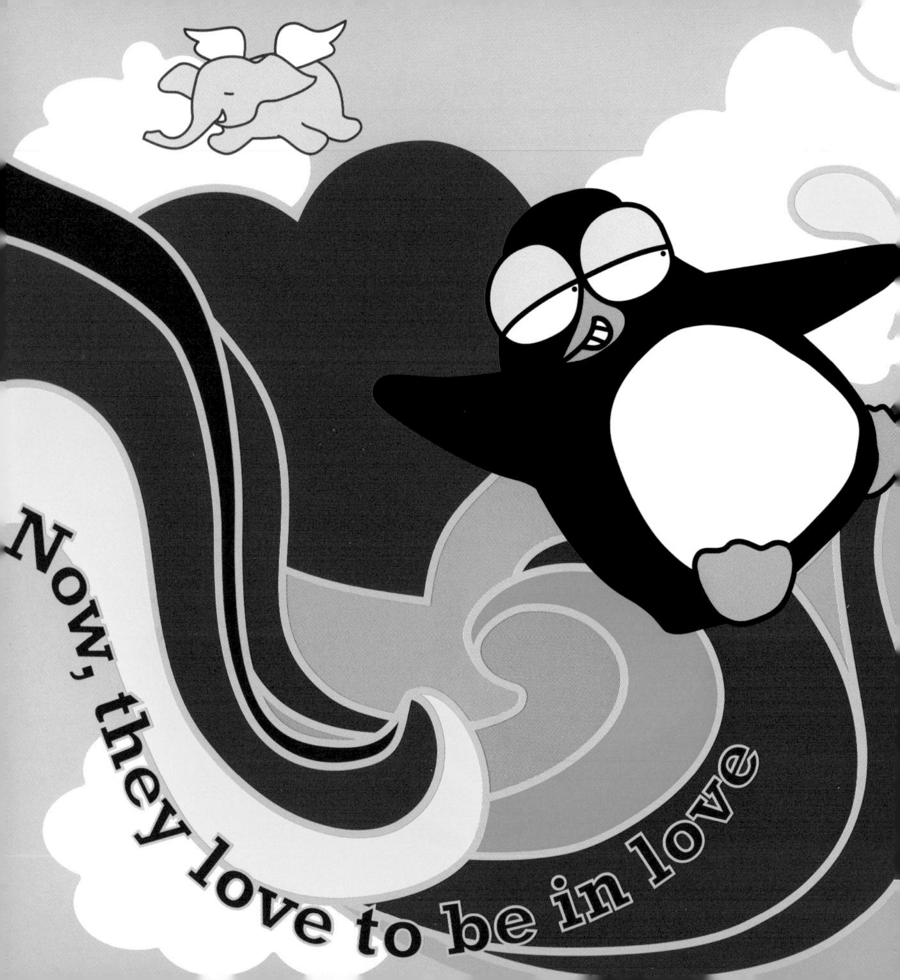

Now, they love to be in love

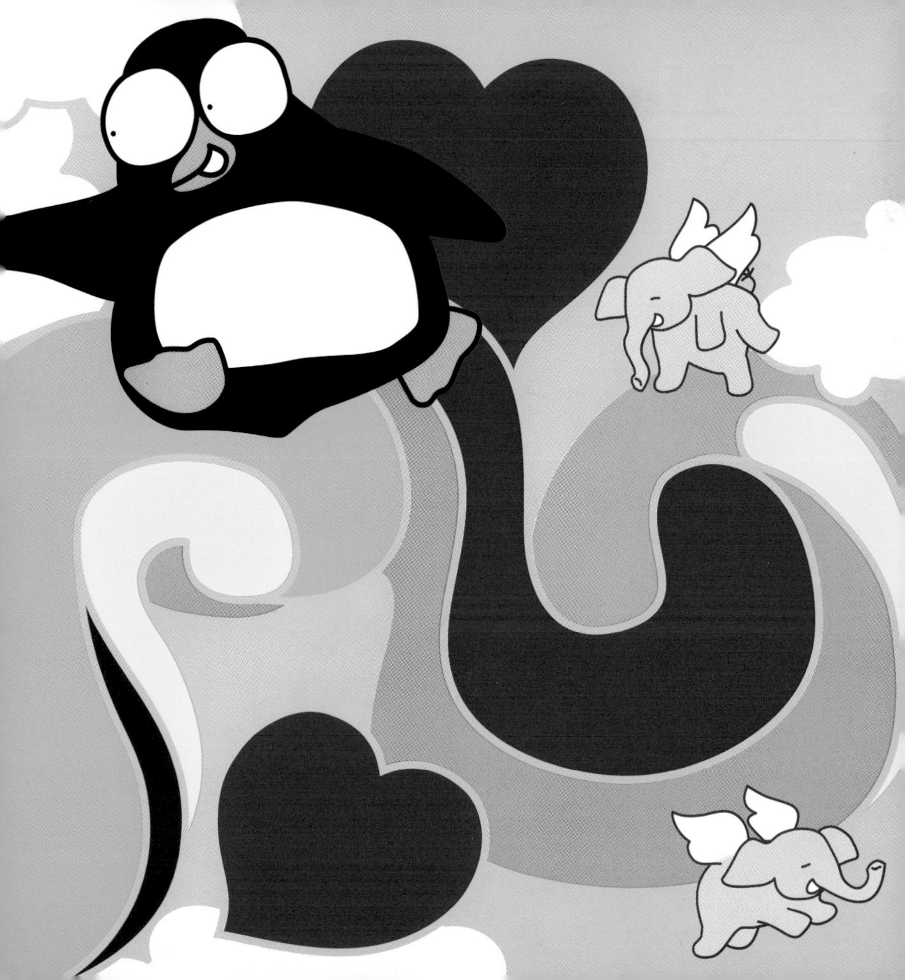

They love each other day

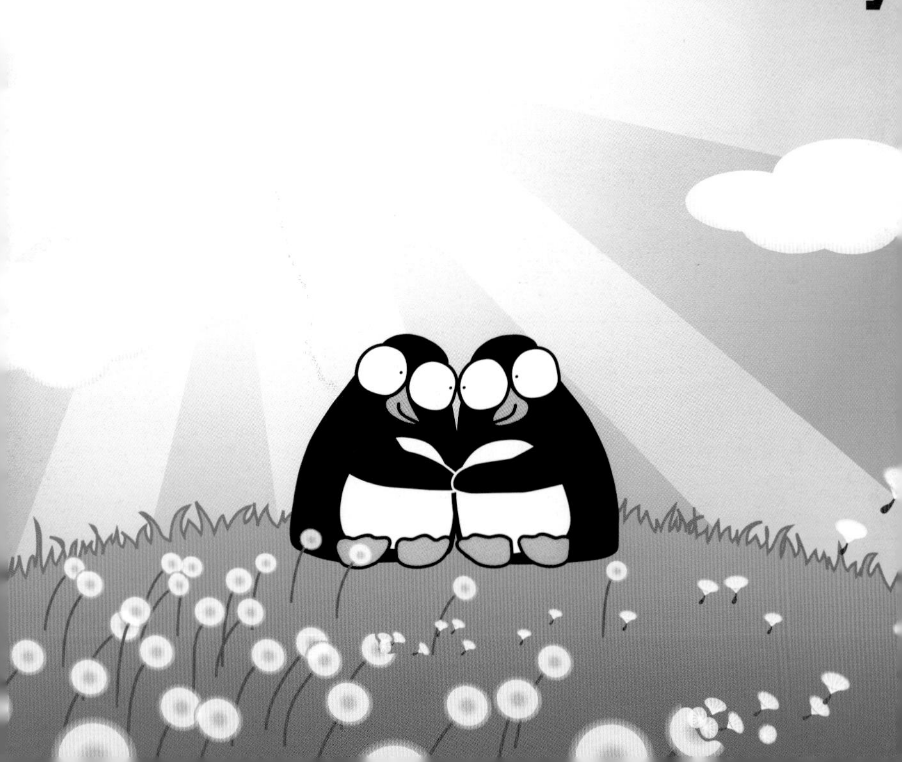

and night

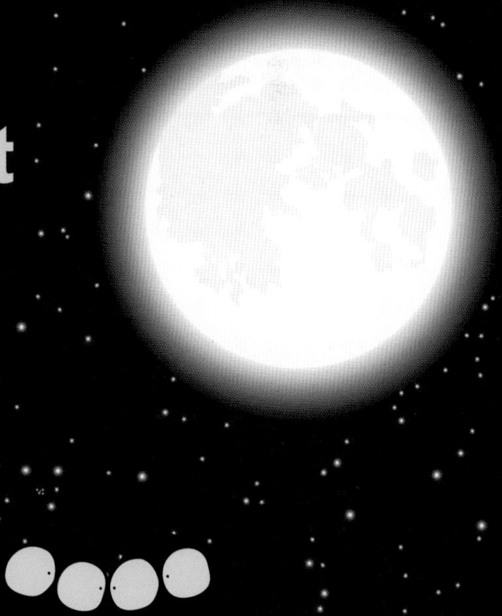

They love each other summer

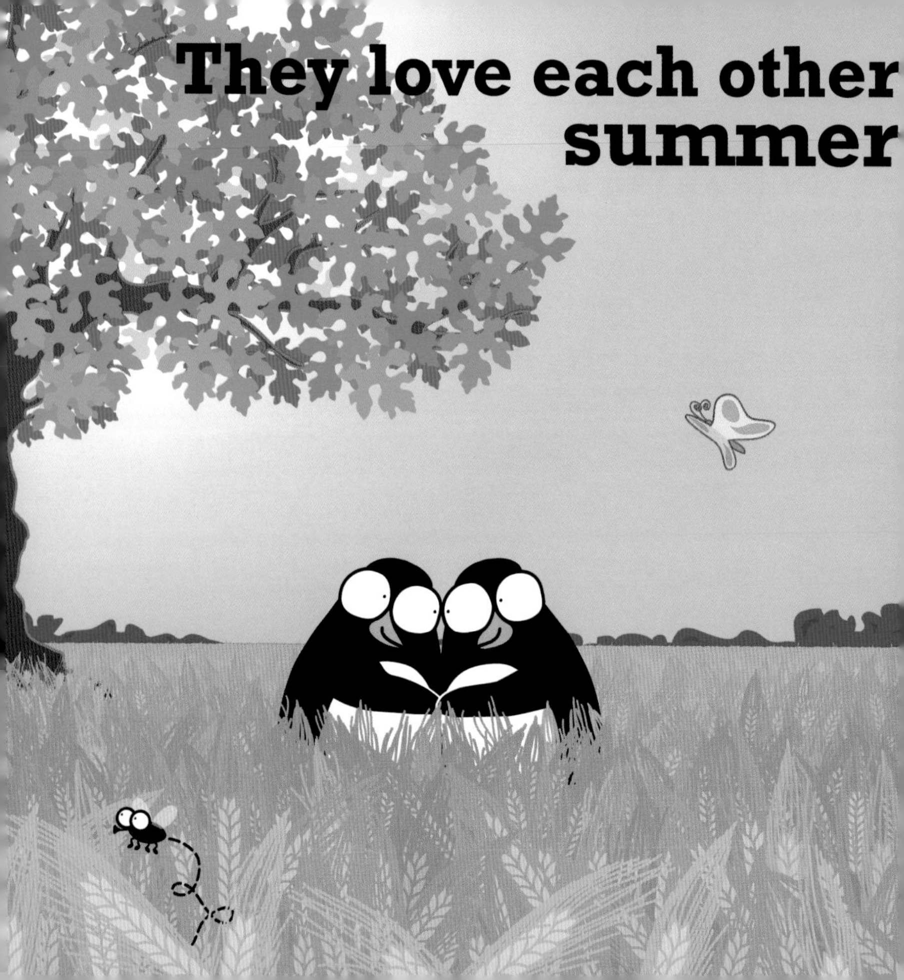

and winter

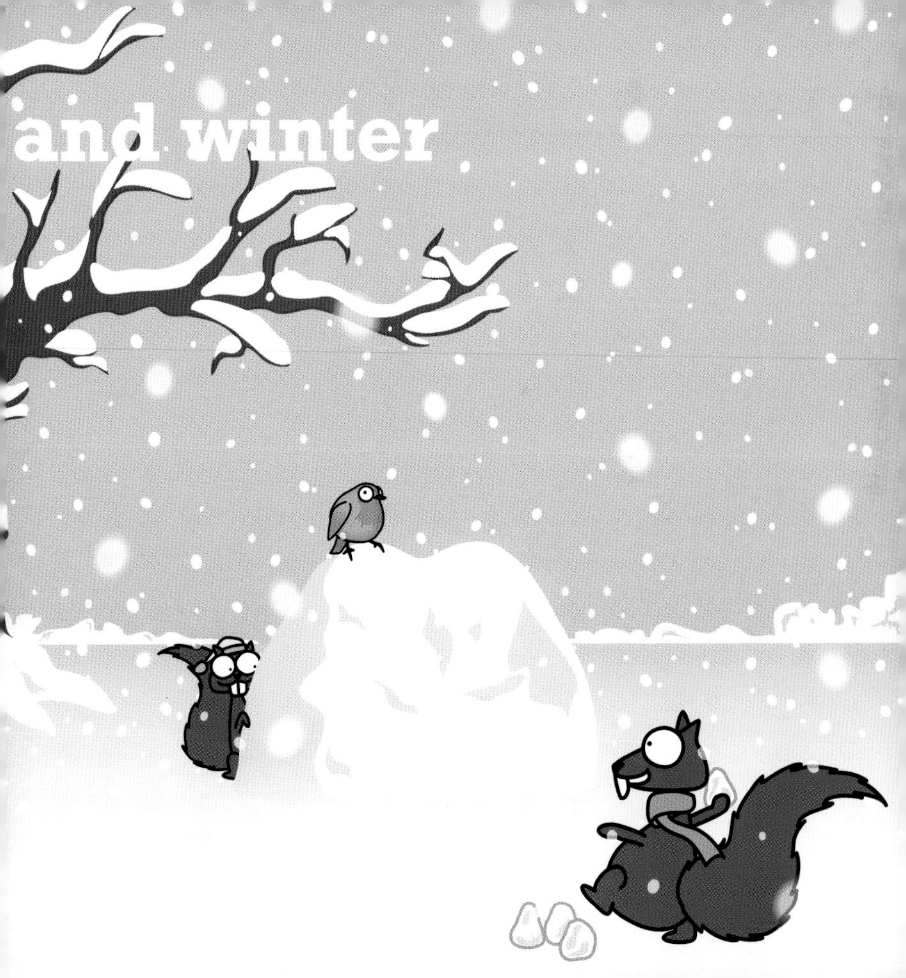

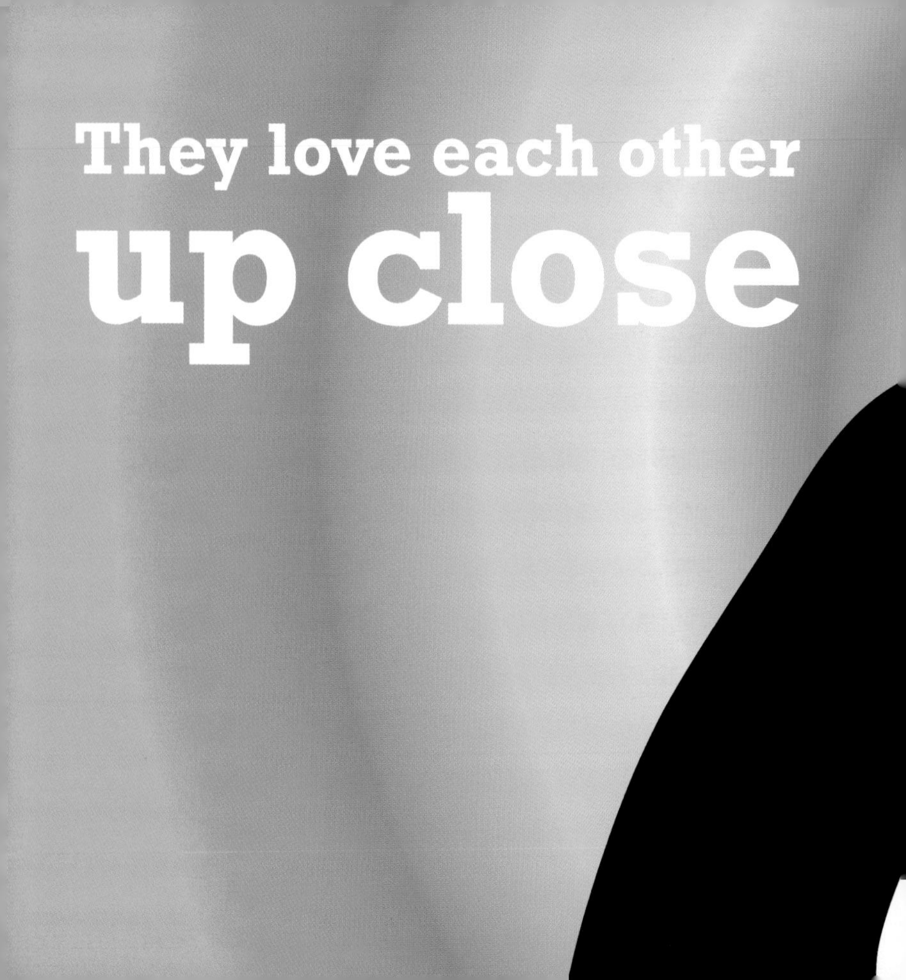
They love each other
up close

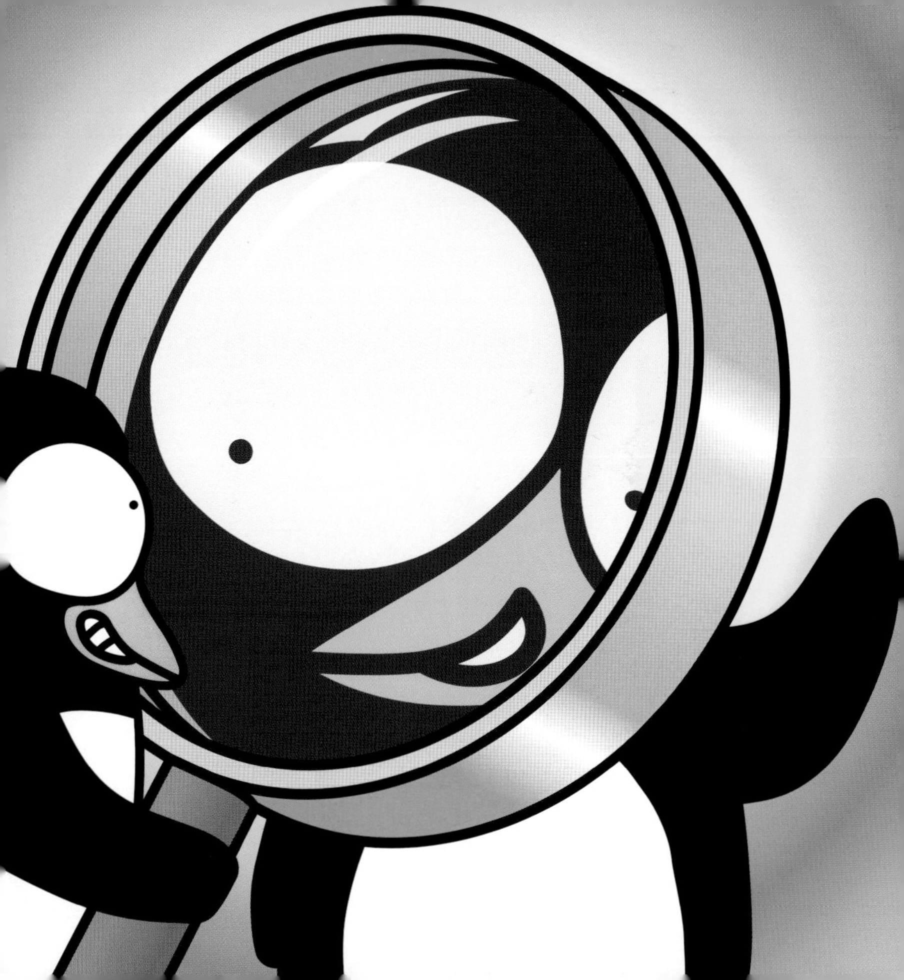

They love each other far apart

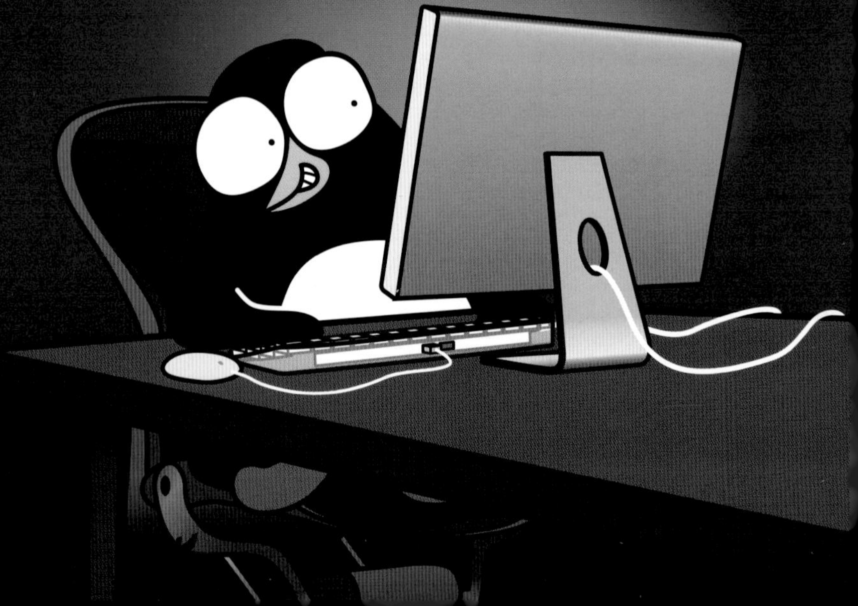

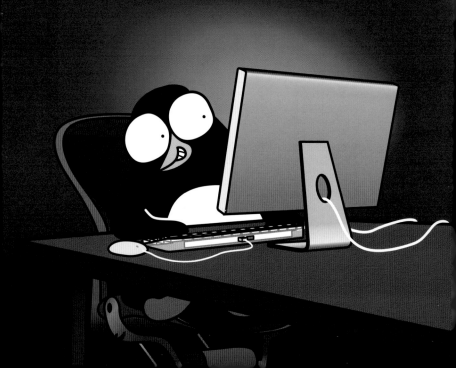

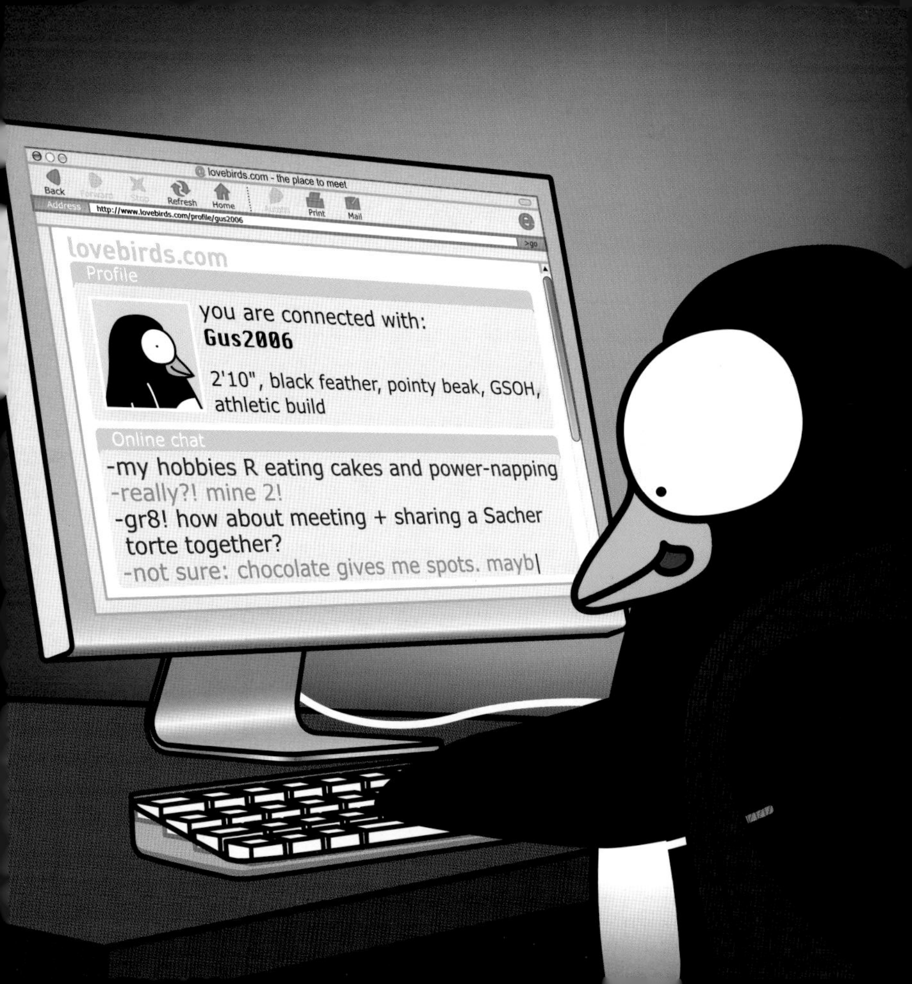
lovebirds.com - the place to meet
Back
Refresh
Home
Print
Mail
Address
http://www.lovebirds.com/profile/gus2006
lovebirds.com
Profile
you are connected with:
Gus2006
2'10", black feather, pointy beak, GSOH, athletic build
Online chat
-my hobbies R eating cakes and power-napping
-really?! mine 2!
-gr8! how about meeting + sharing a Sacher torte together?
-not sure: chocolate gives me spots. mayb

They love each other

CLUCK!
EXCLUSIVE
HENRIETTA'S
BLAH BLAH
WC

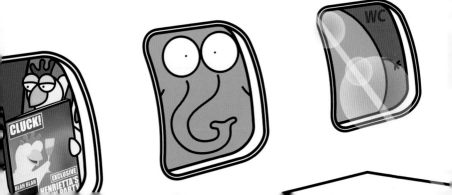

sky high

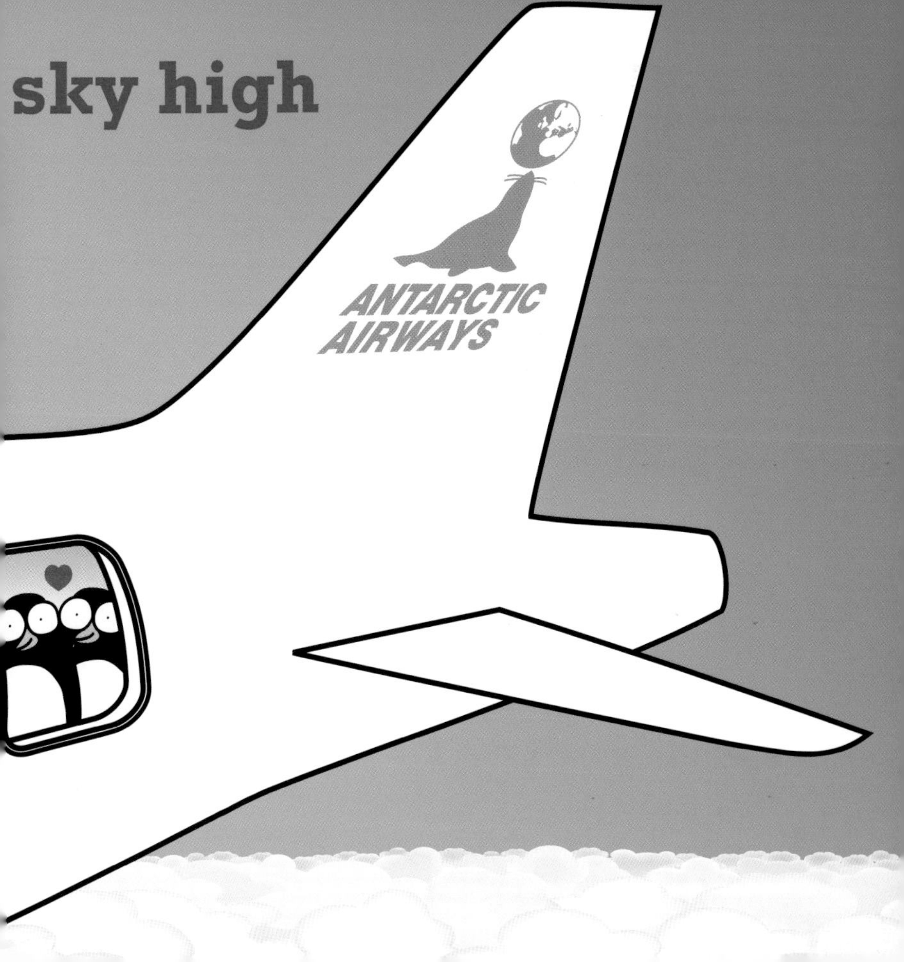
ANTARCTIC
AIRWAYS

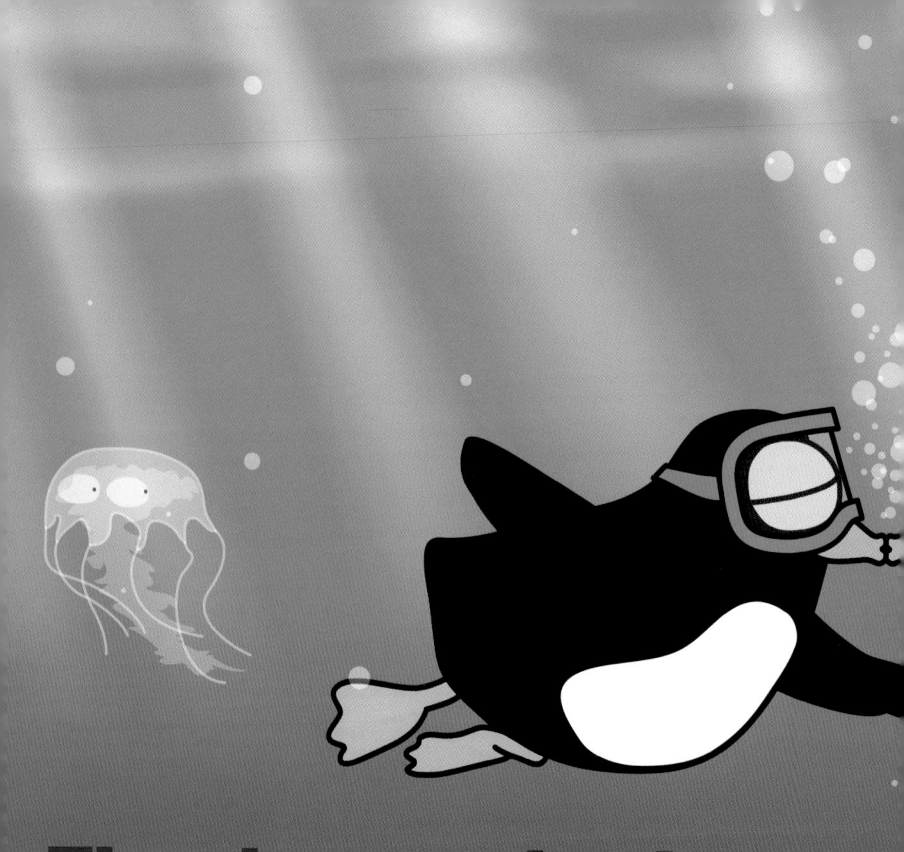

They love each other
deep

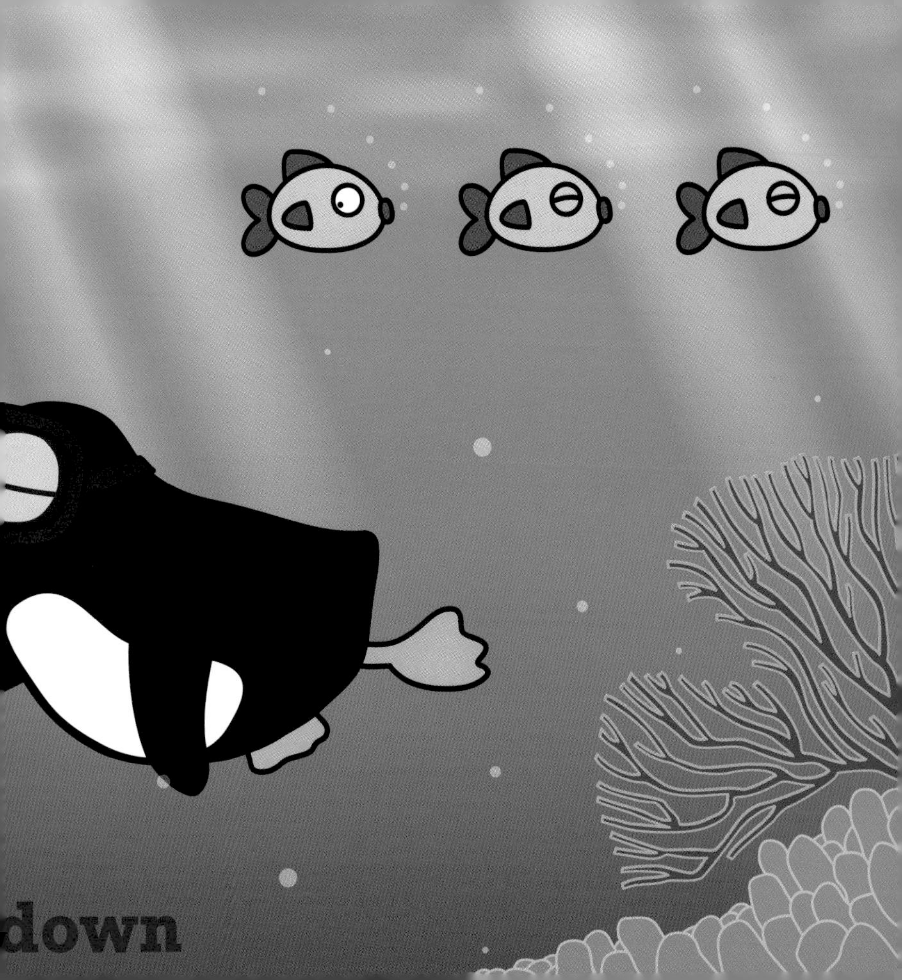

down

They love each other sweetly

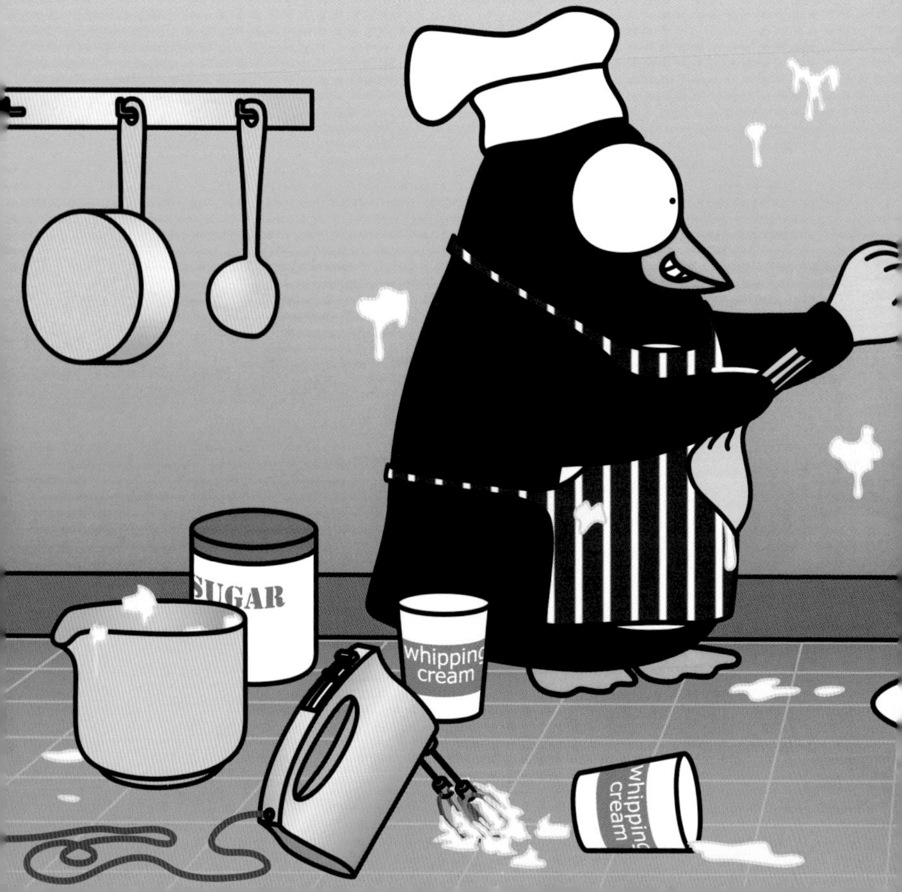
SUGAR
whipping cream
whipping cream

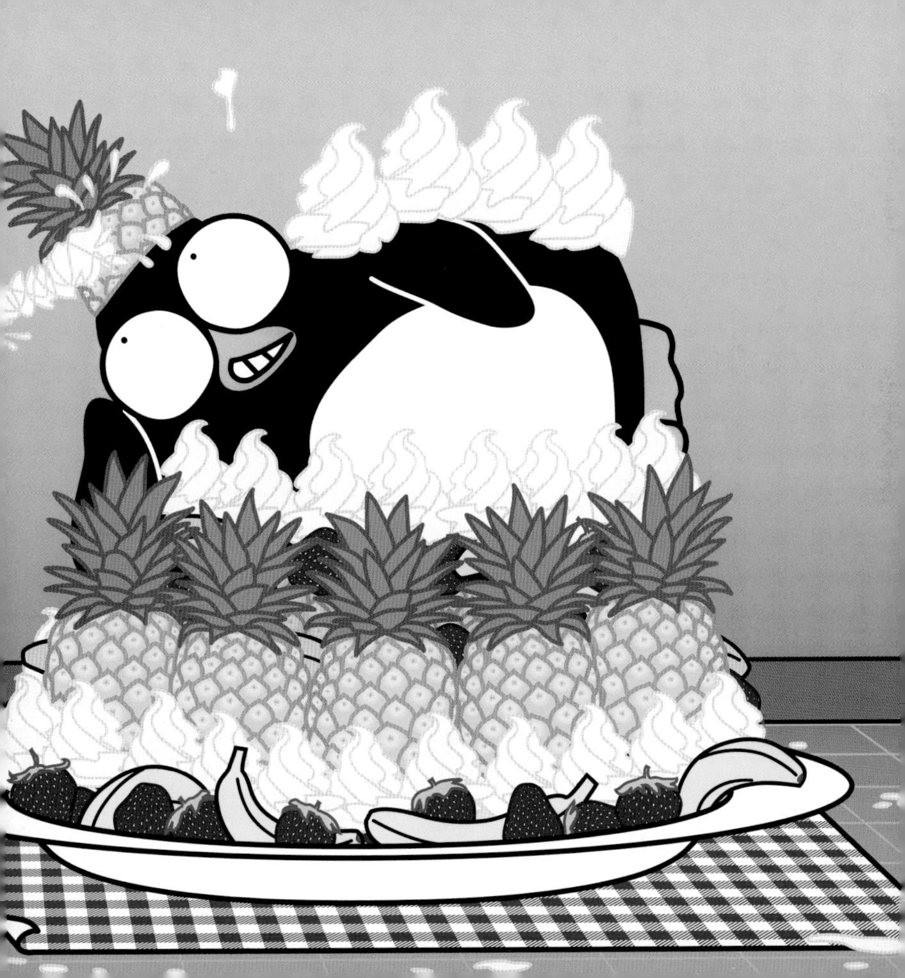

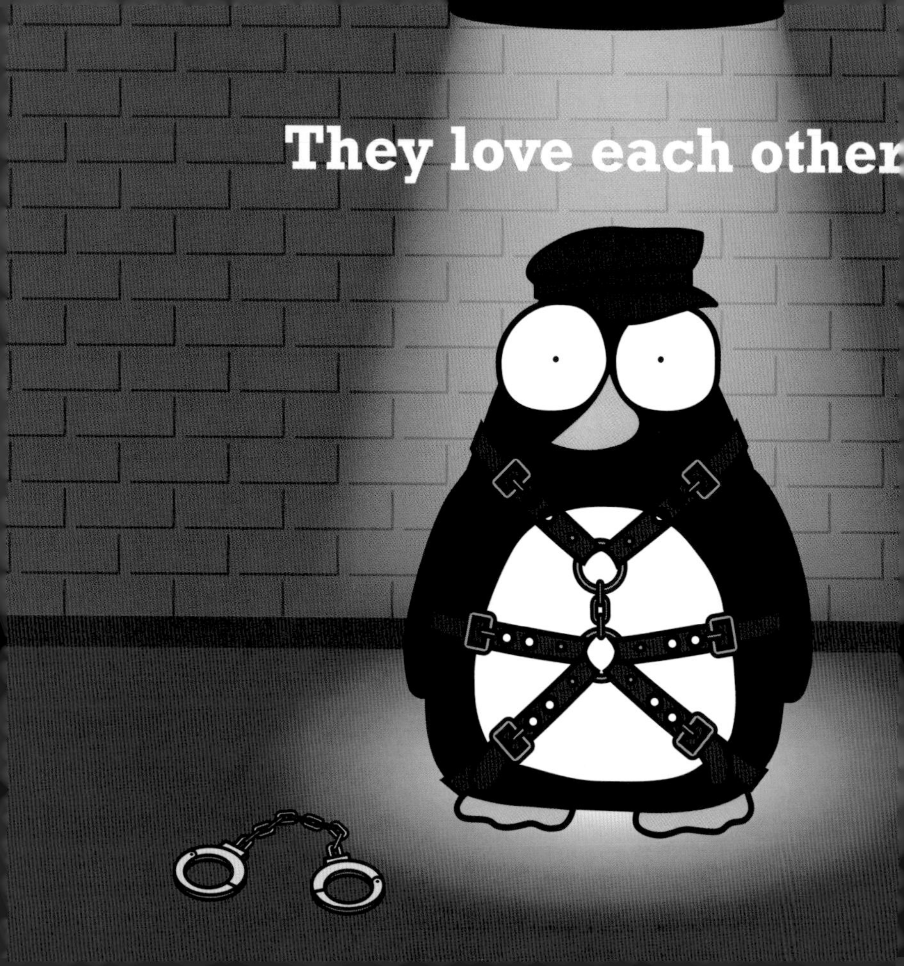

They love each other

with a dash of spice

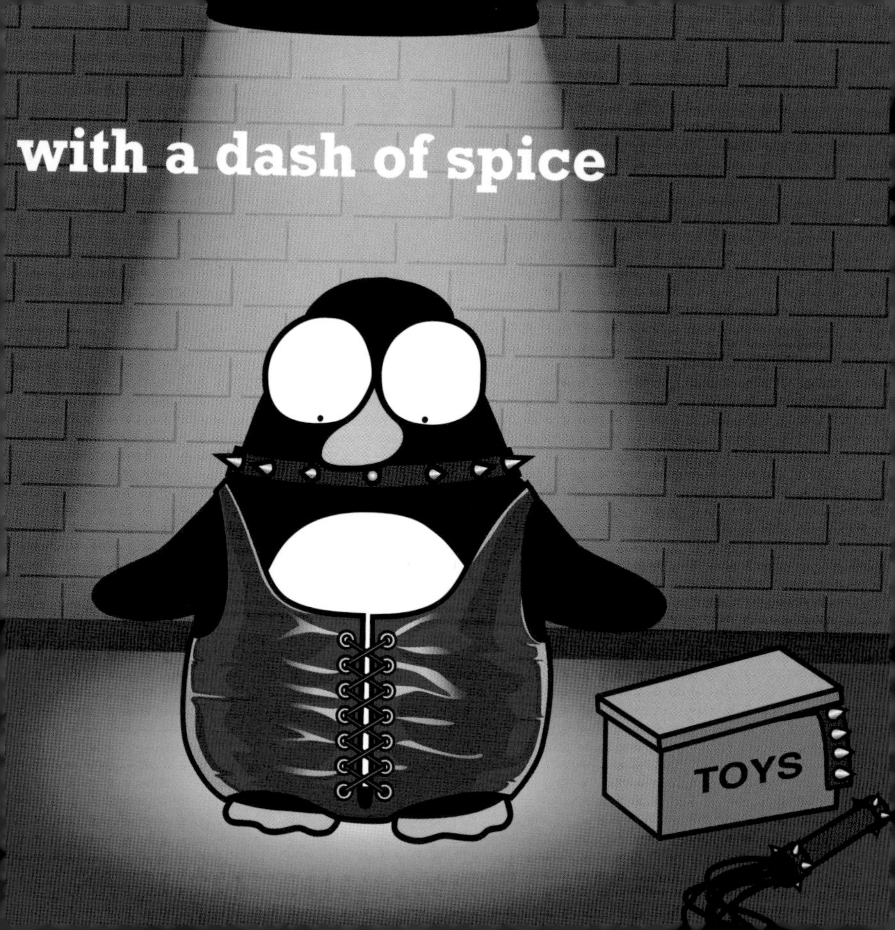
TOYS

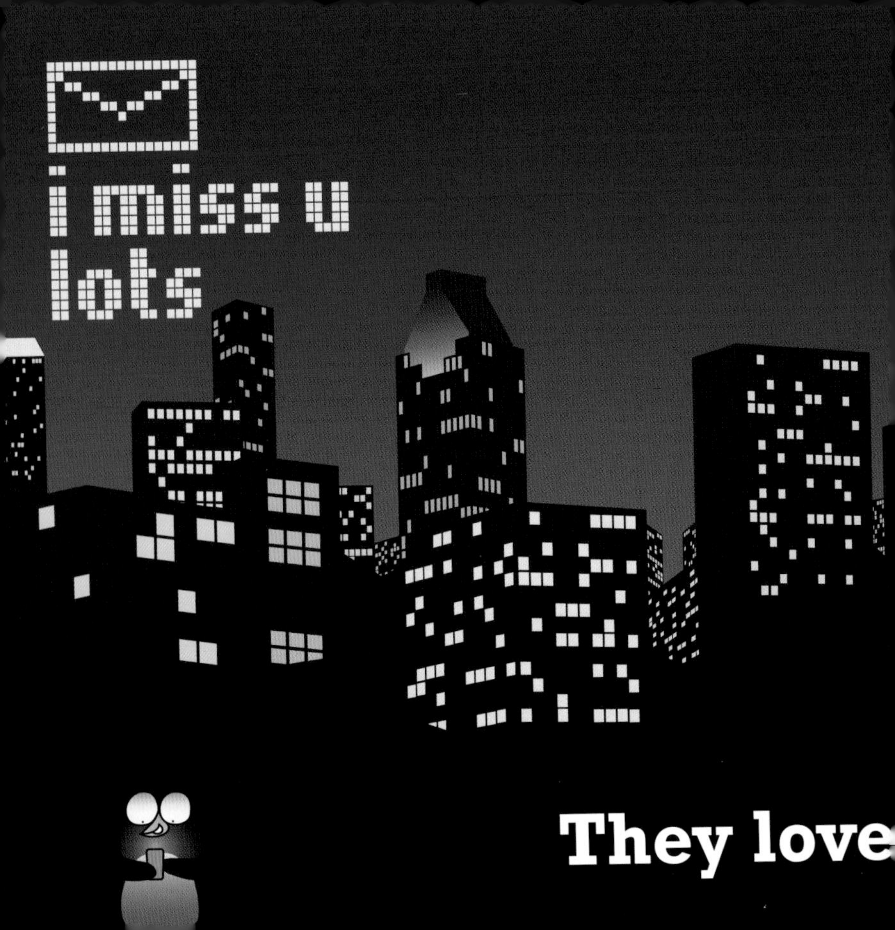
i miss u
lots

They love

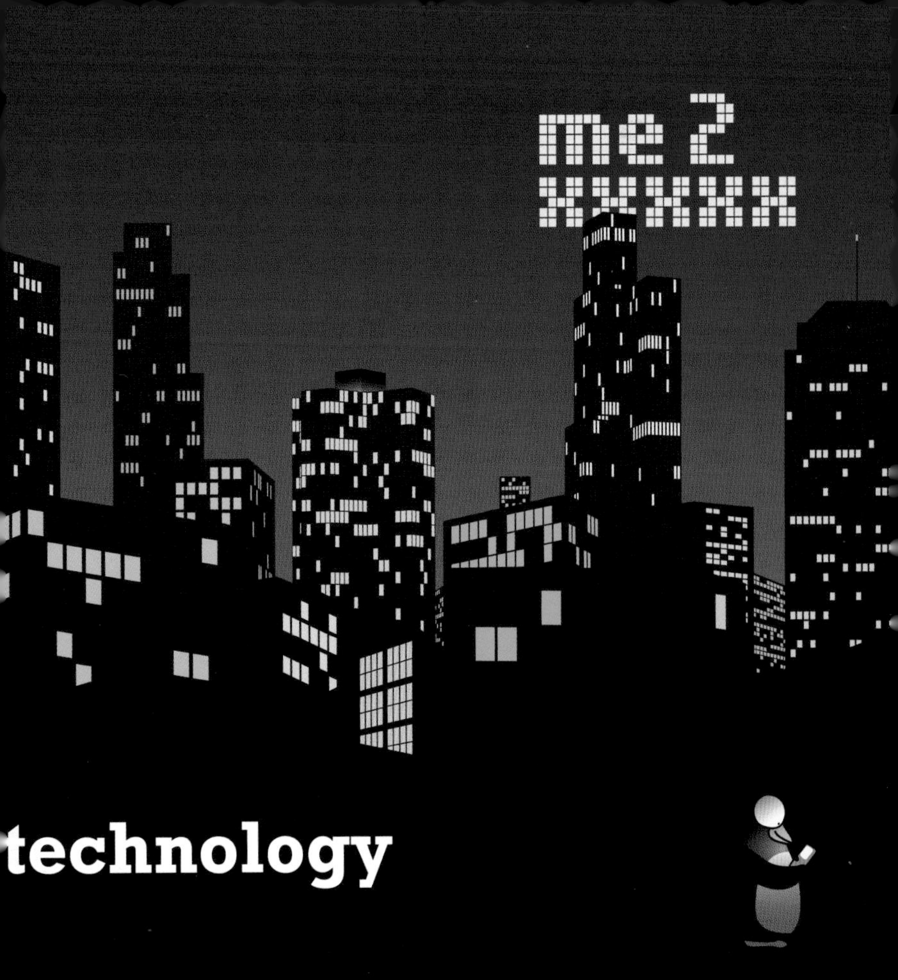
me 2
xxxxxx

technology

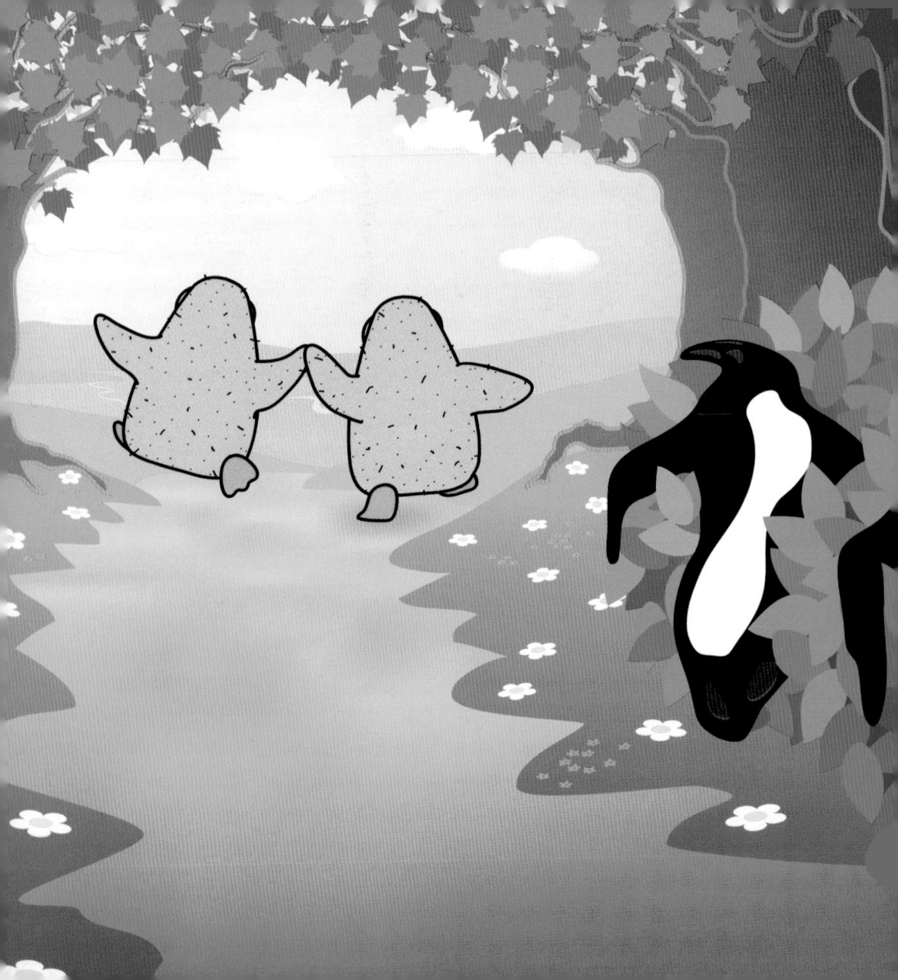

They love nature

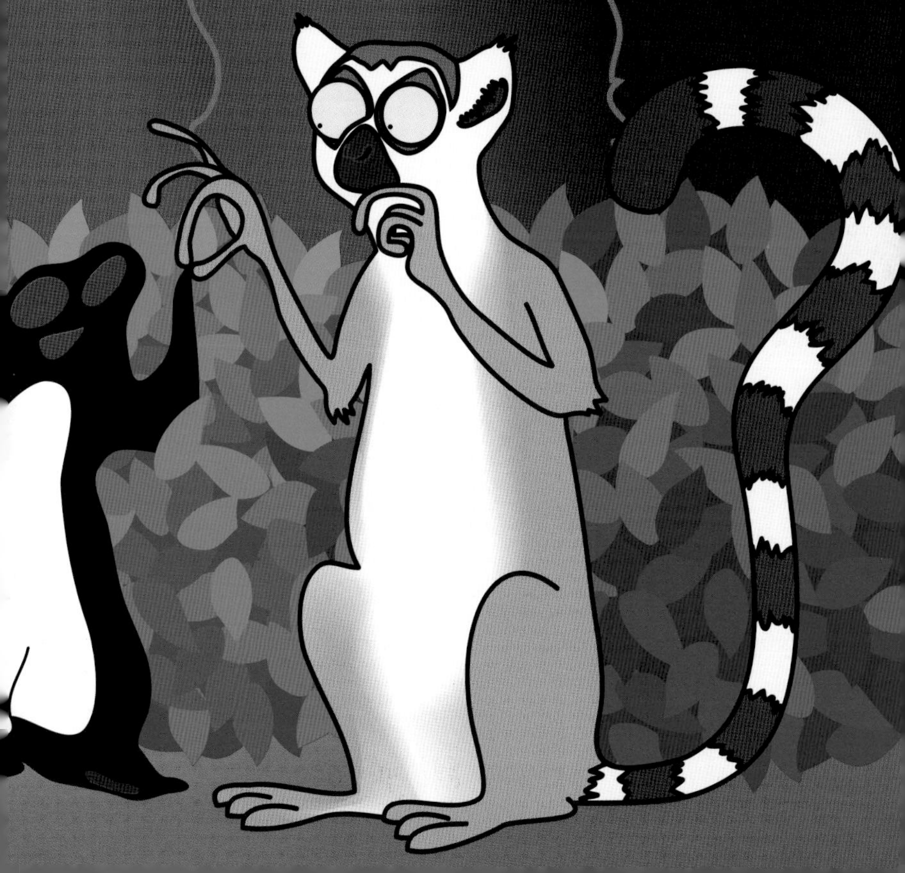

They love being bubbly

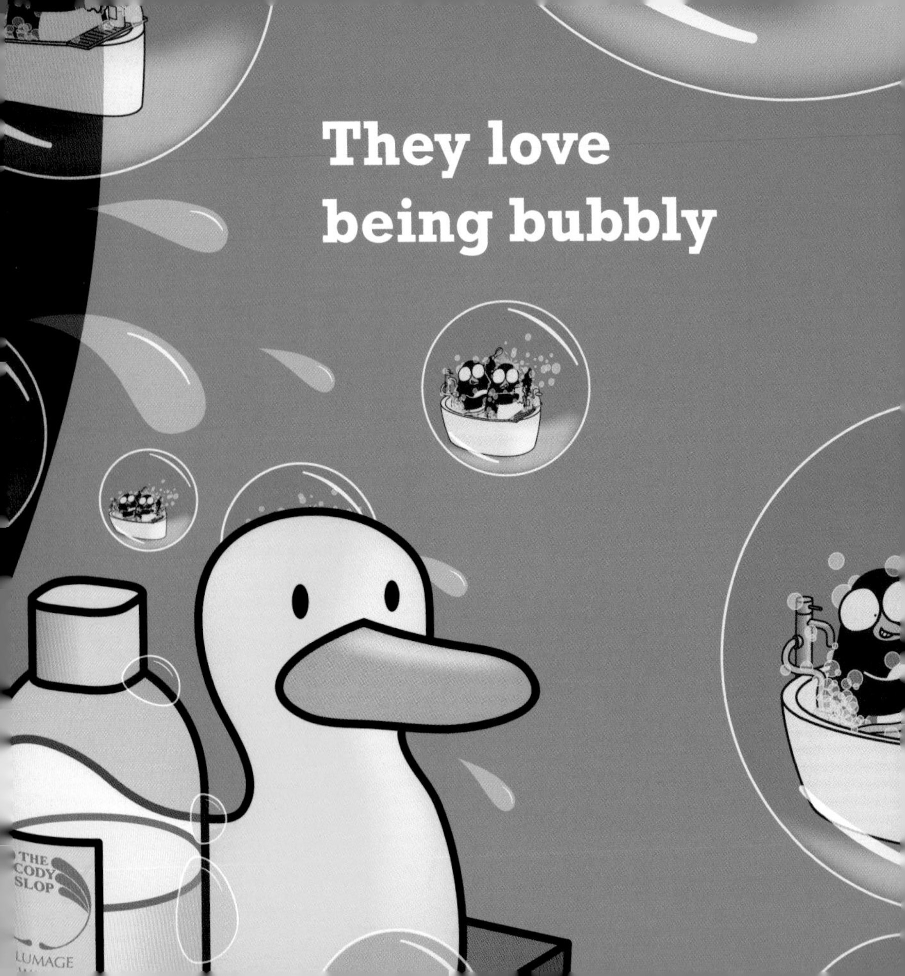
THE
CODY
SLOP
LUMAGE

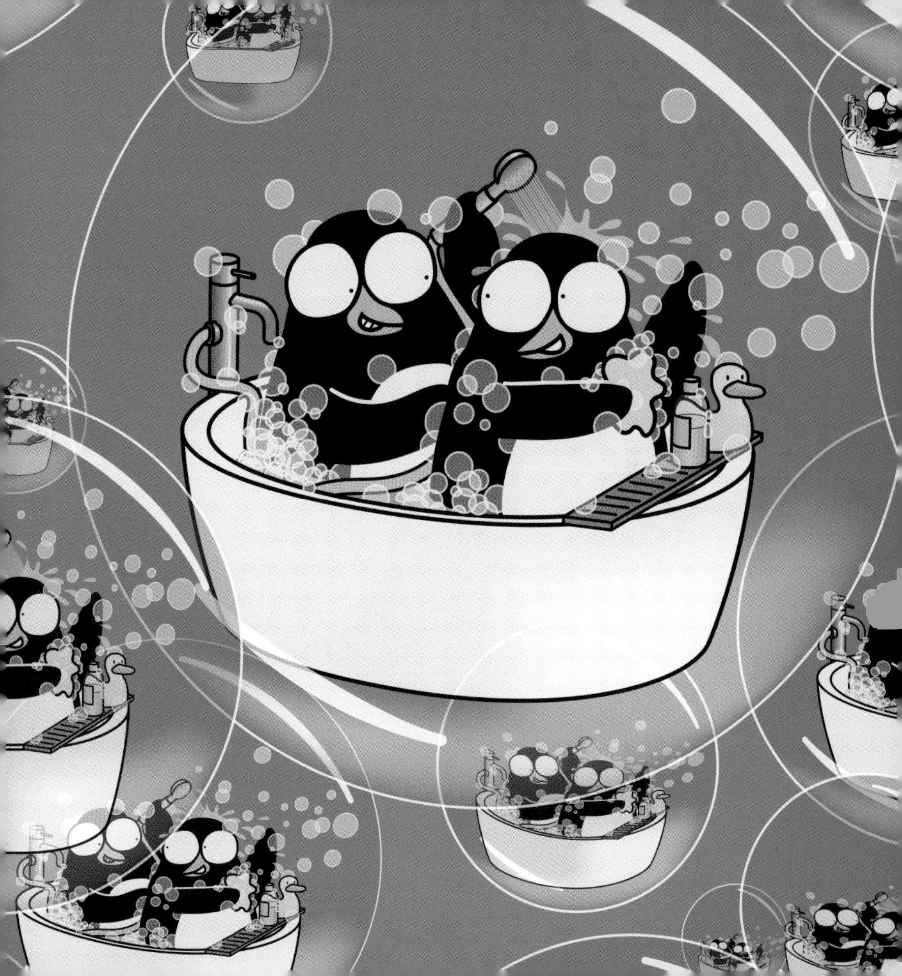

They love their lava lamp

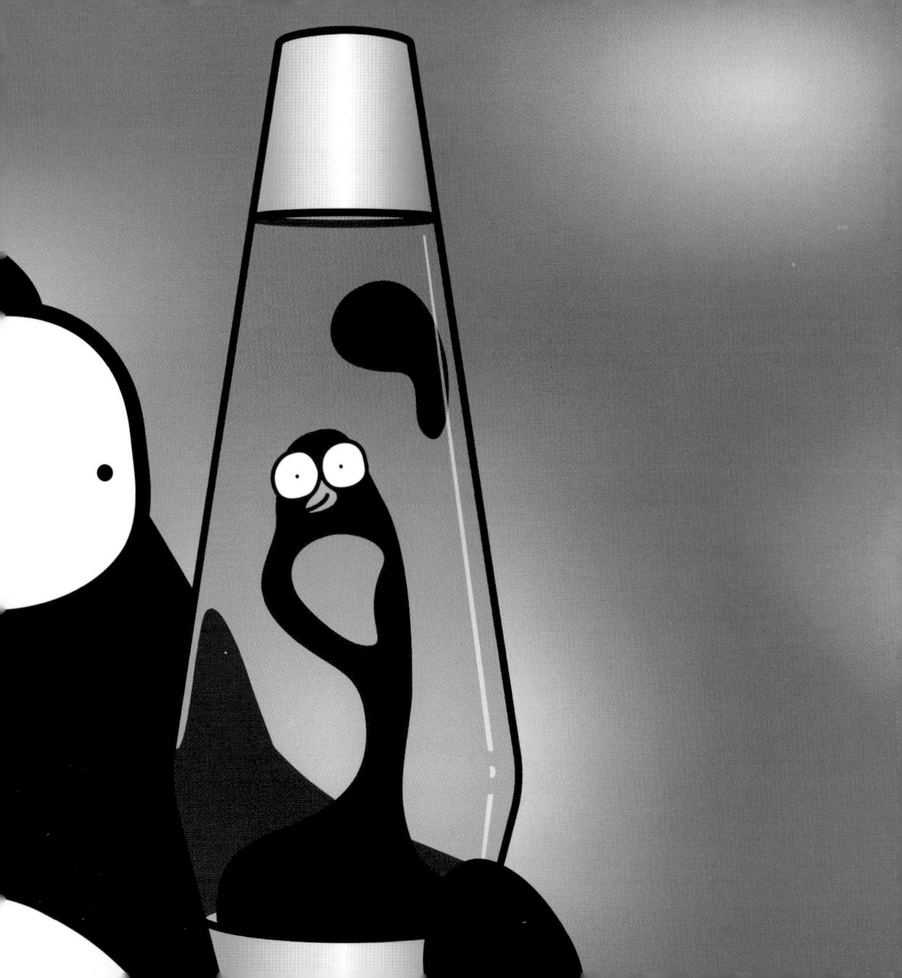

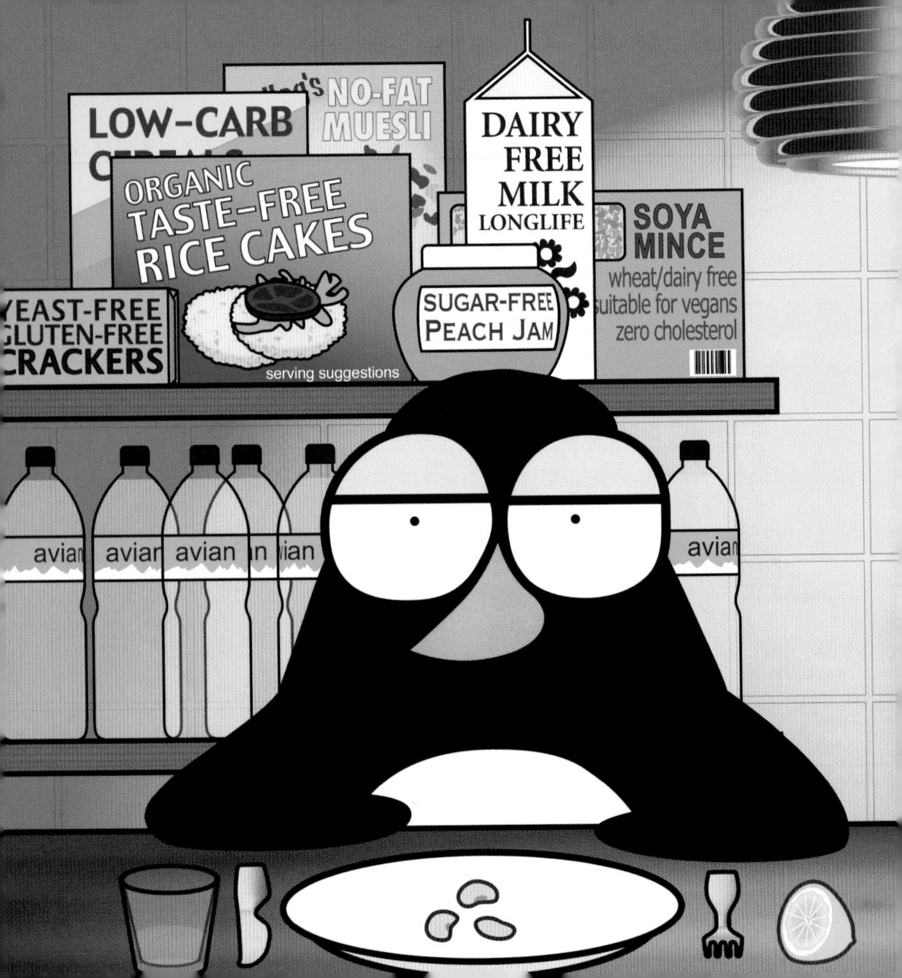
LOW-CARB
NO-FAT MUESLI
ORGANIC TASTE-FREE RICE CAKES
serving suggestions
YEAST-FREE GLUTEN-FREE CRACKERS
DAIRY FREE MILK LONGLIFE
SUGAR-FREE PEACH JAM
SOYA MINCE
wheat/dairy free
suitable for vegans
zero cholesterol
avian

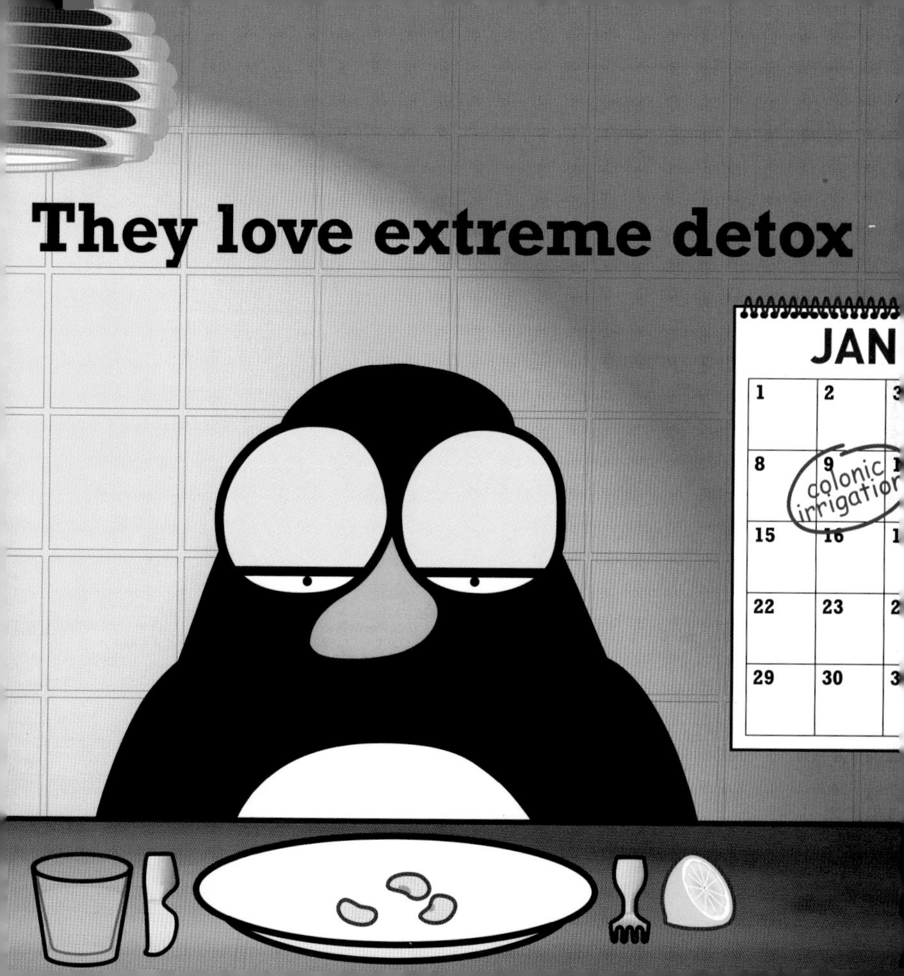
JAN
1
2
8
9
colonic irrigation
15
16
22
23
29
30

They love extreme detox

They love extreme re-tox

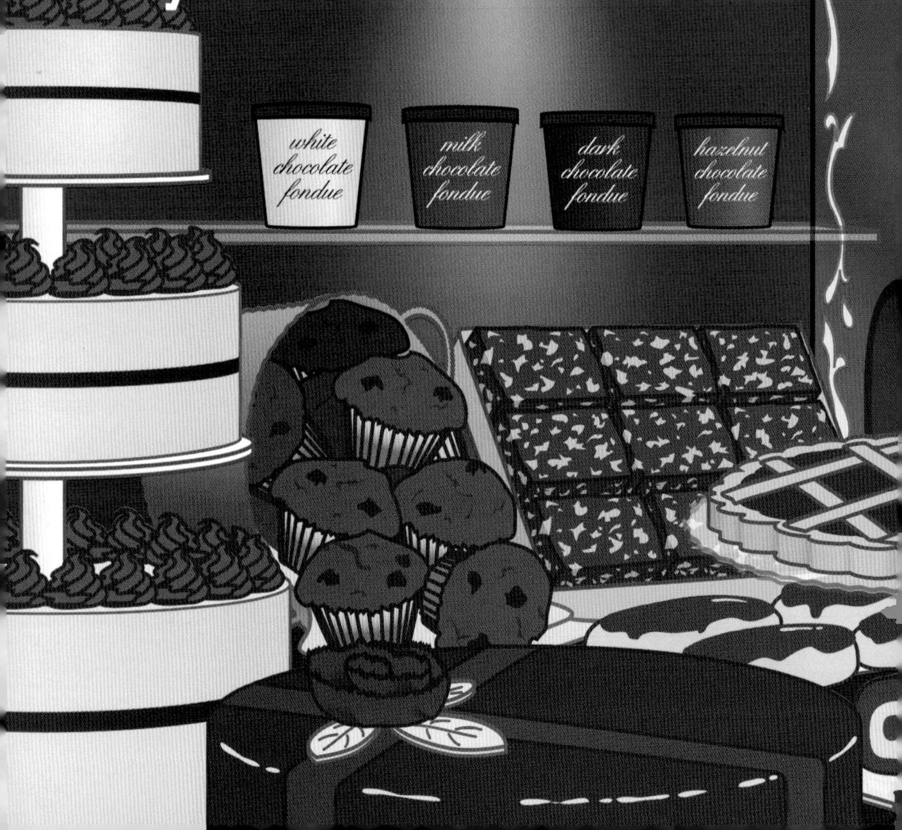
white chocolate fondue
milk chocolate fondue
dark chocolate fondue
hazelnut chocolate fondue

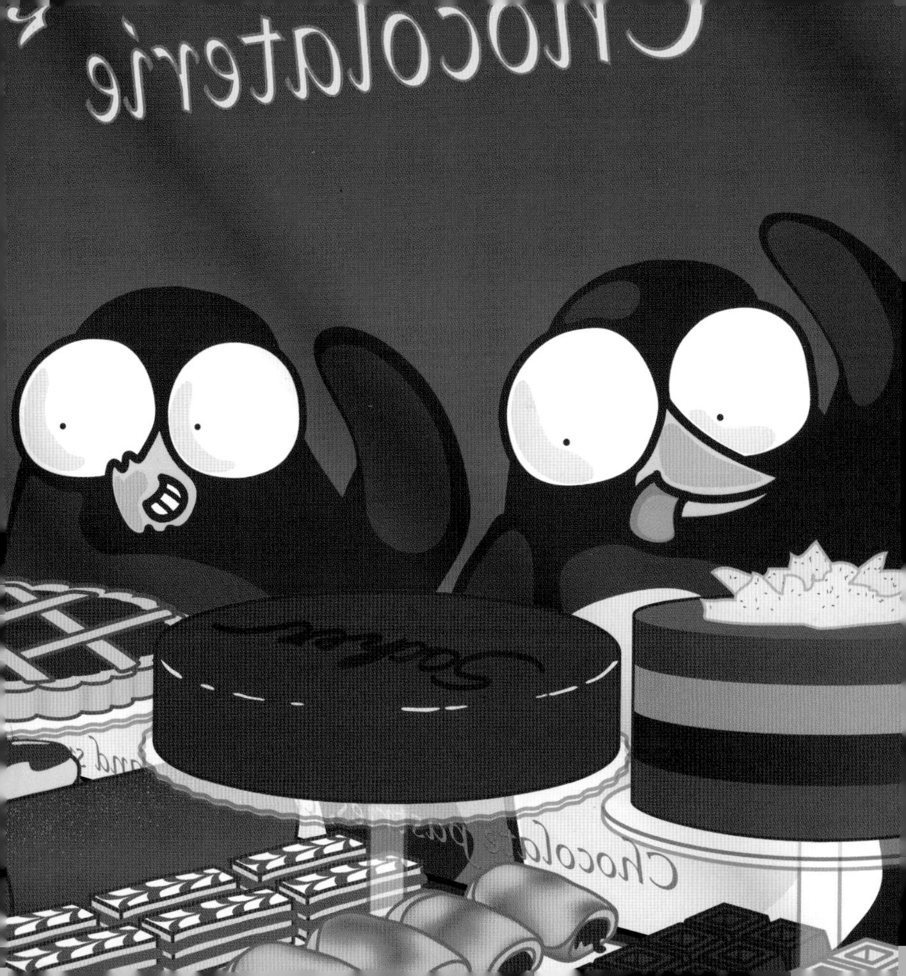
Chocolaterie

They love

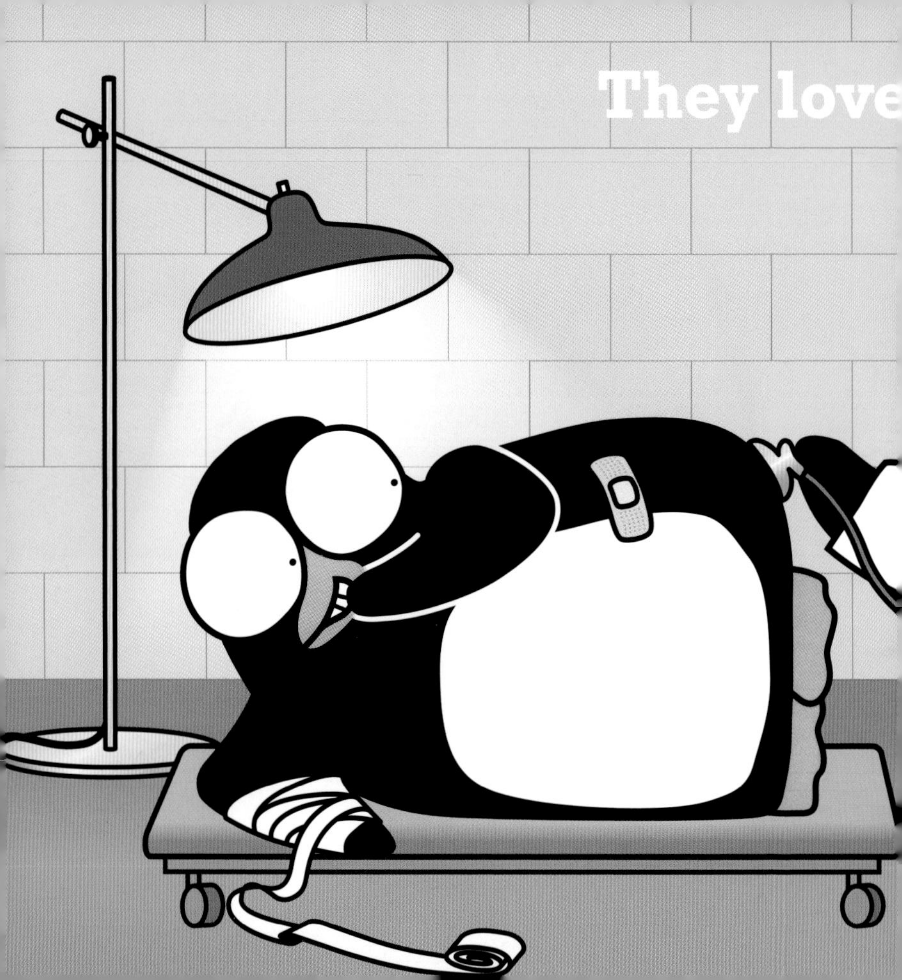

THE PENGUIN BODY

Pectorals

Skull

Deltoids

Ribs

Abs

Fat

Spine

PATIENT: Waldo

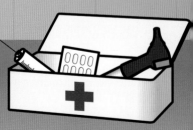

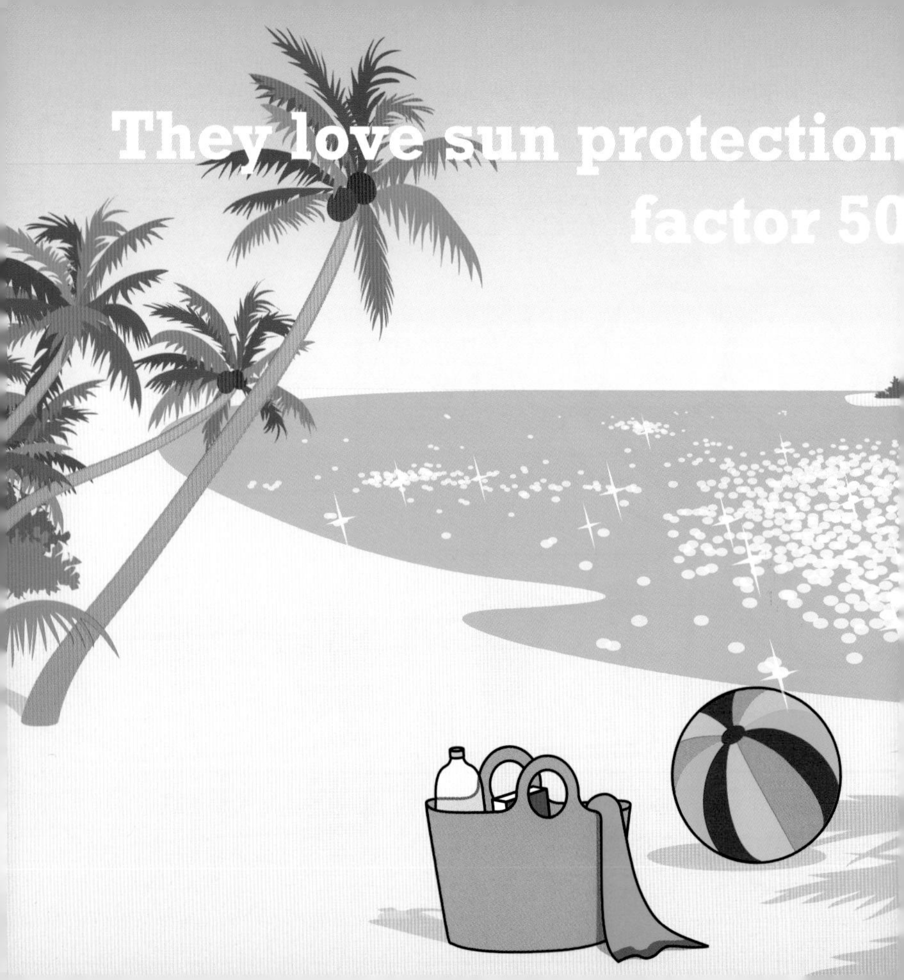
They love sun protection
factor 50

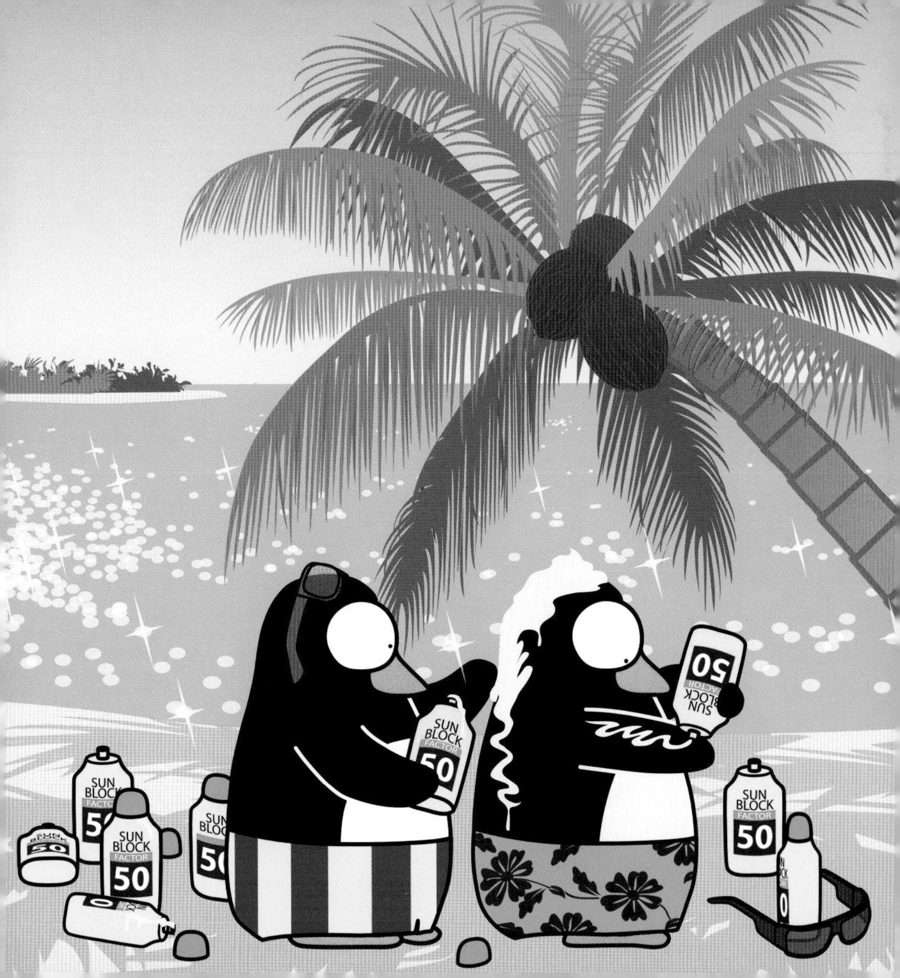
SUN BLOCK FACTOR 50
SUN BLOCK FACTOR 50
SUN BLOCK FACTOR 50
SUN BLOCK FACTOR 50
SUN BLOCK FACTOR 50

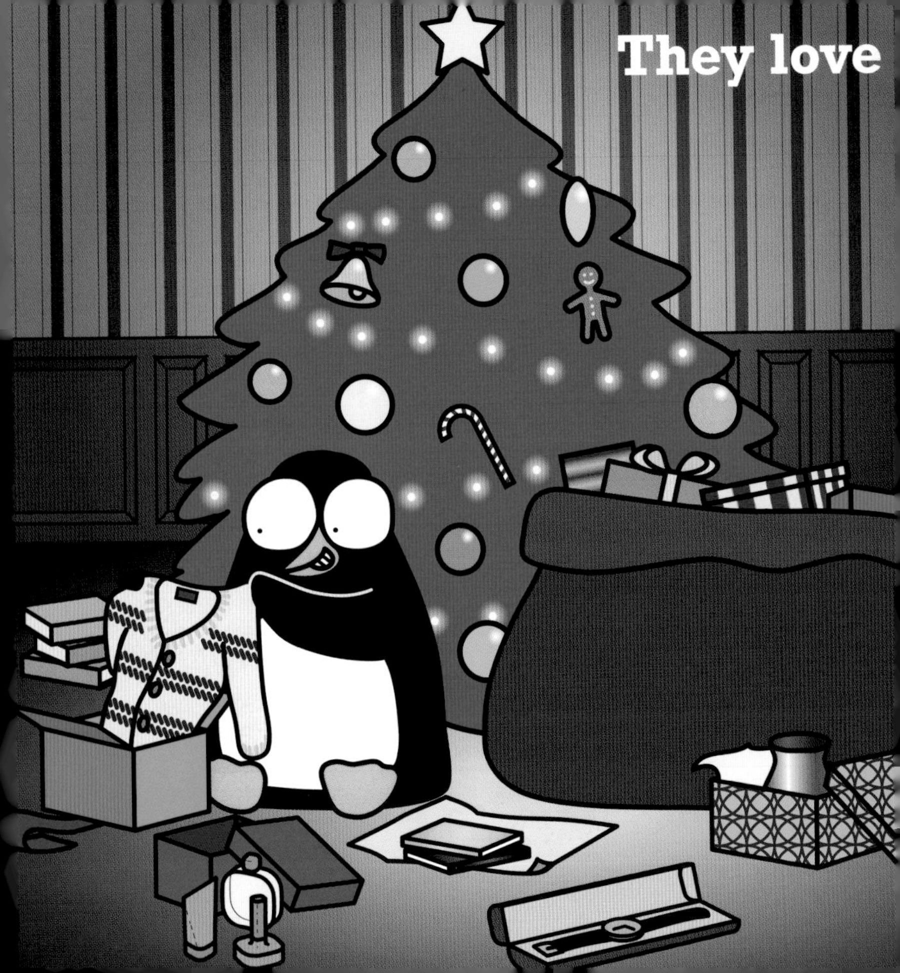
They love

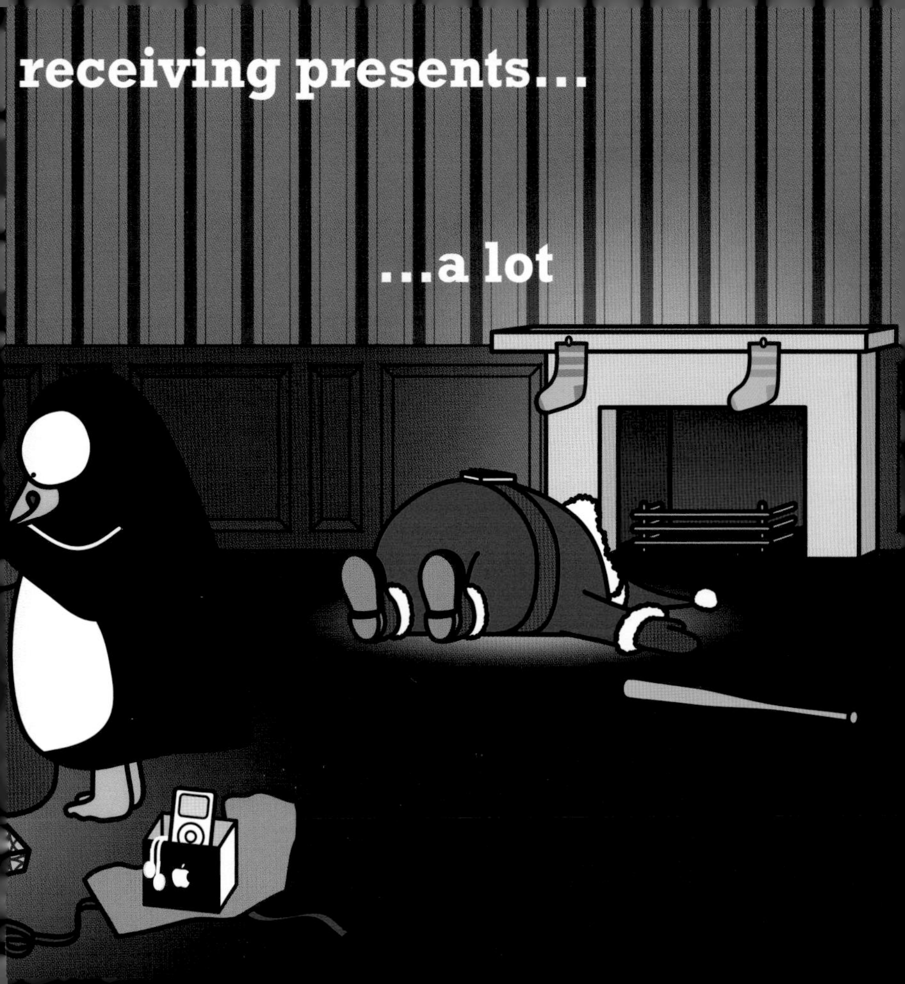
receiving presents...
...a lot

They love 60
and

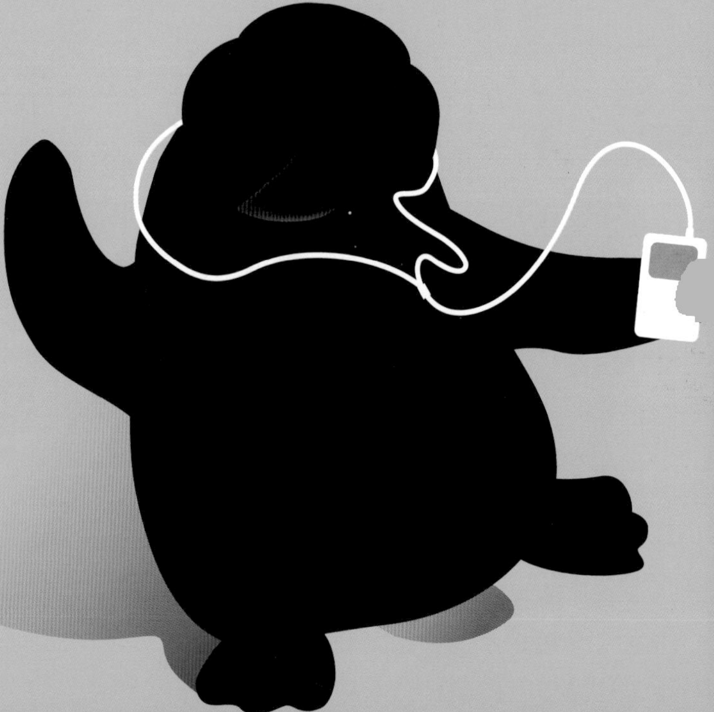

gigabytes
15,000 songs

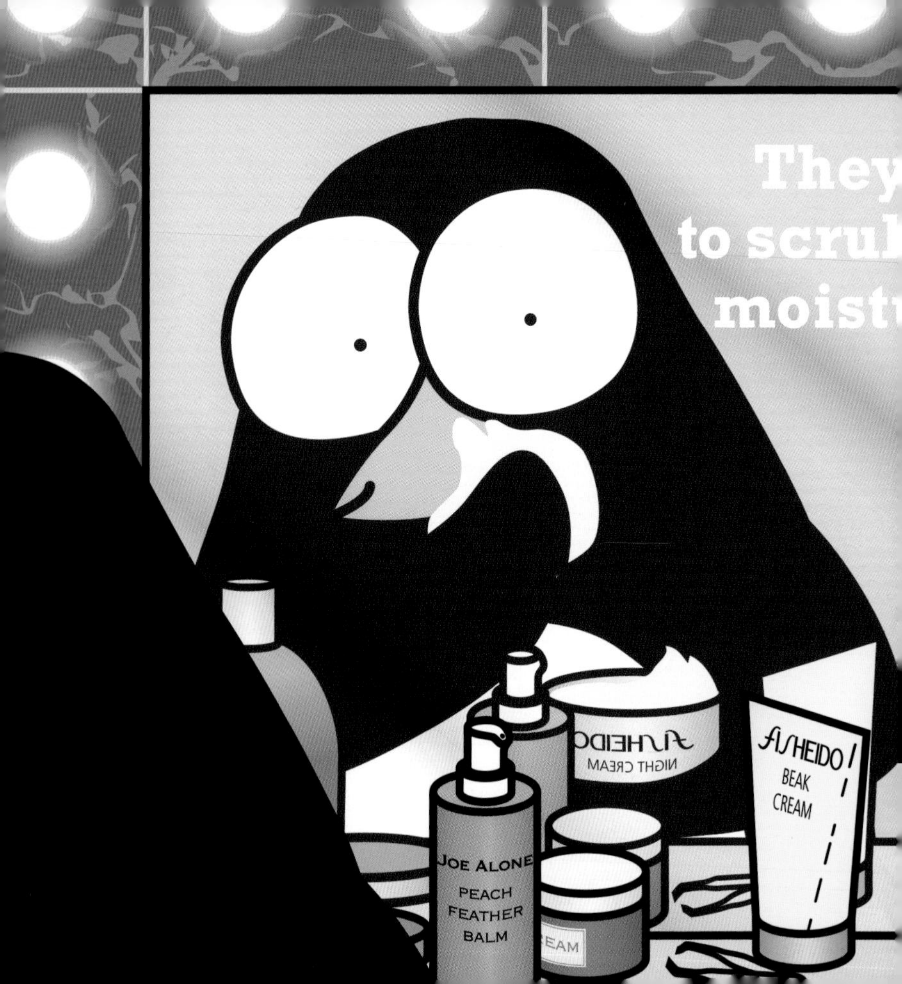
They
to scru
moist
BEAK
CREAM
JOE ALONE
PEACH
FEATHER
BALM
EAM

love
and
rise

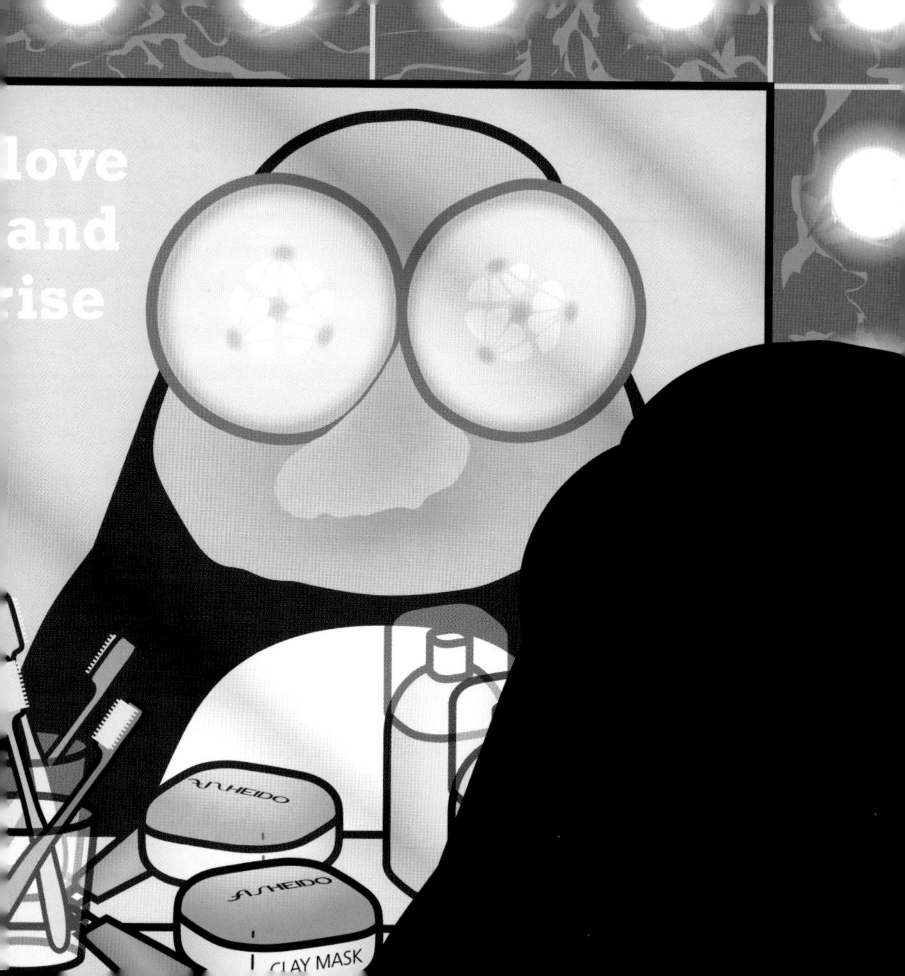
CLAY MASK

They love to feel the

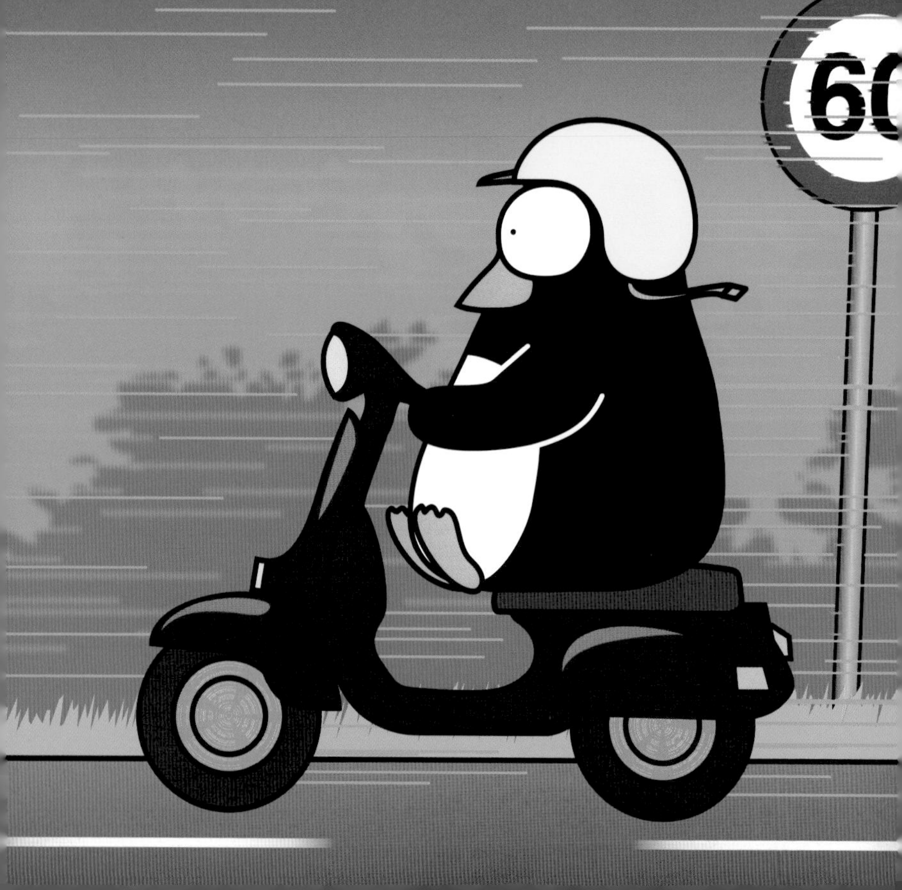
60

wind on their beaks

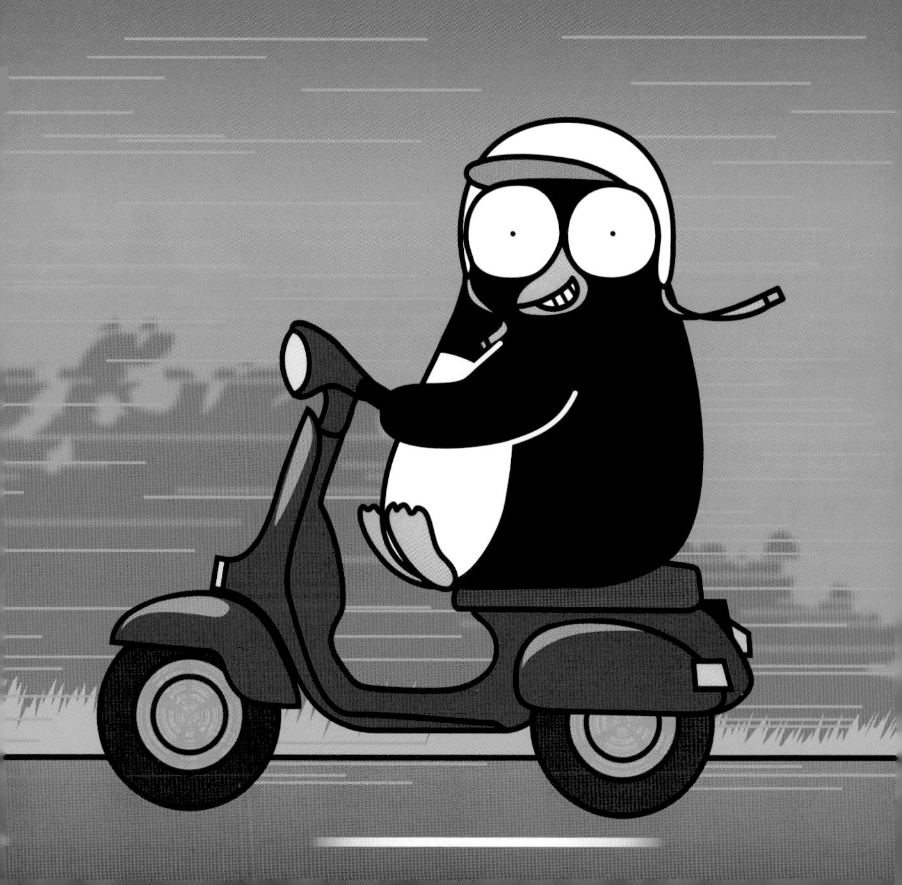

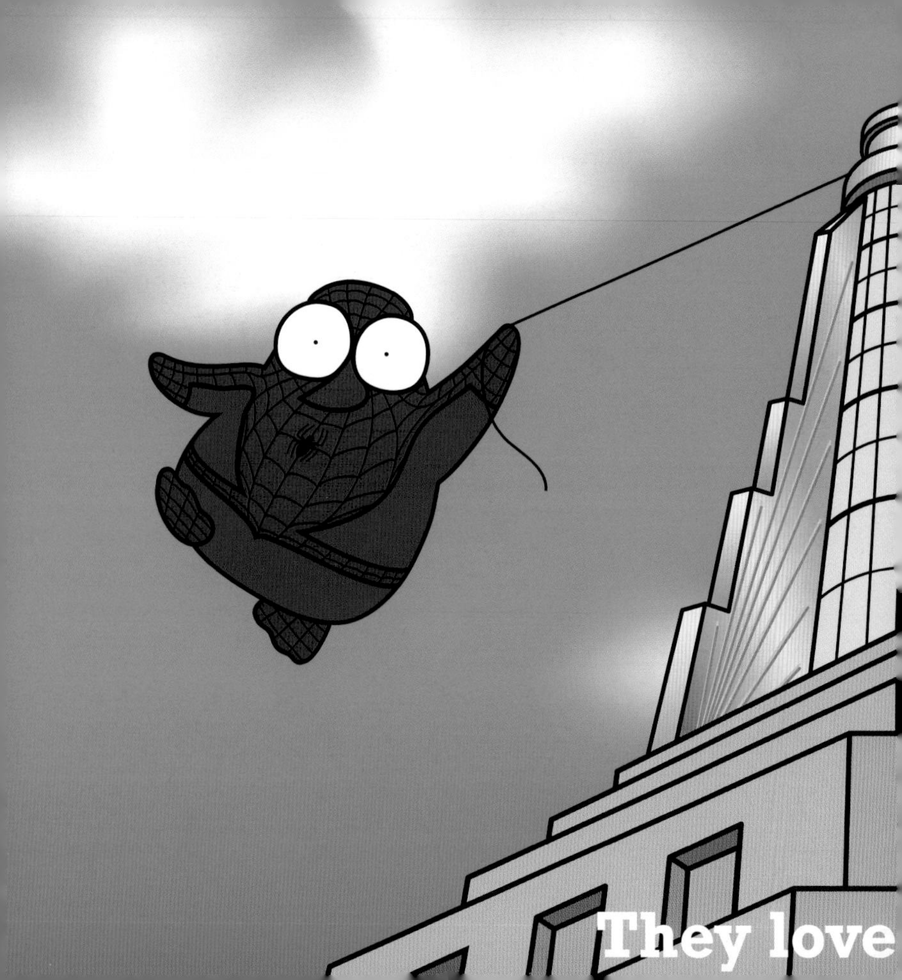

They love

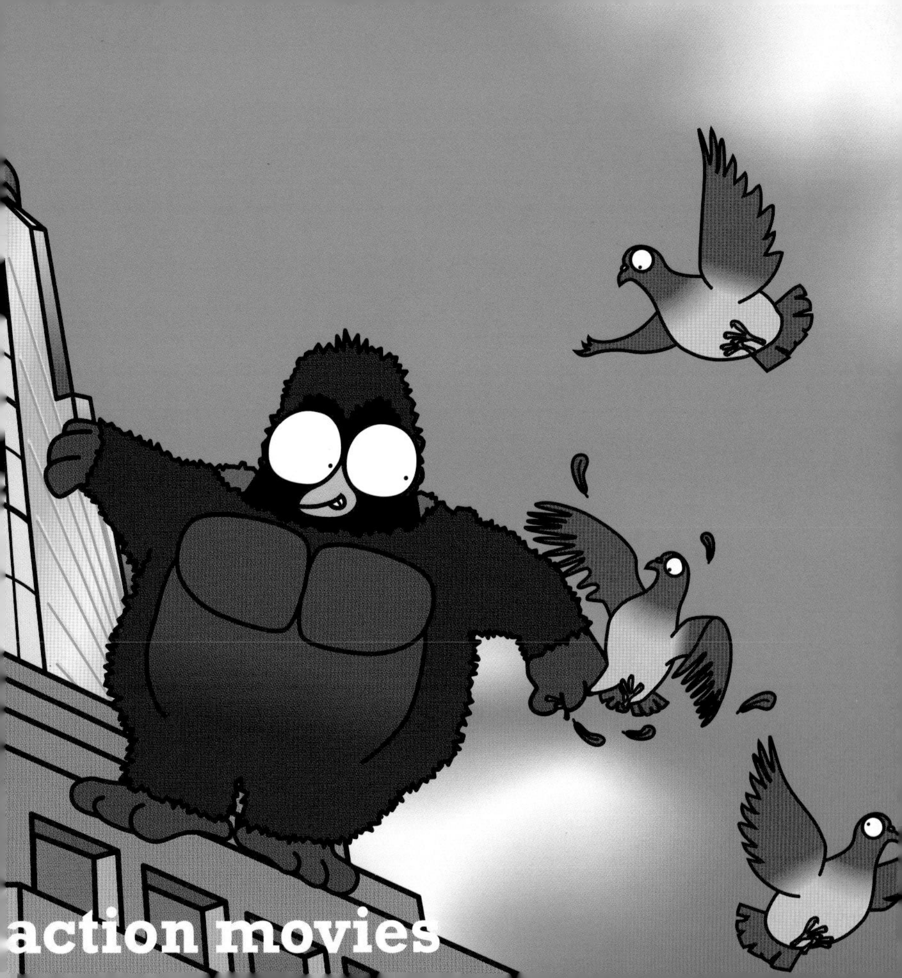

action movies

They love to

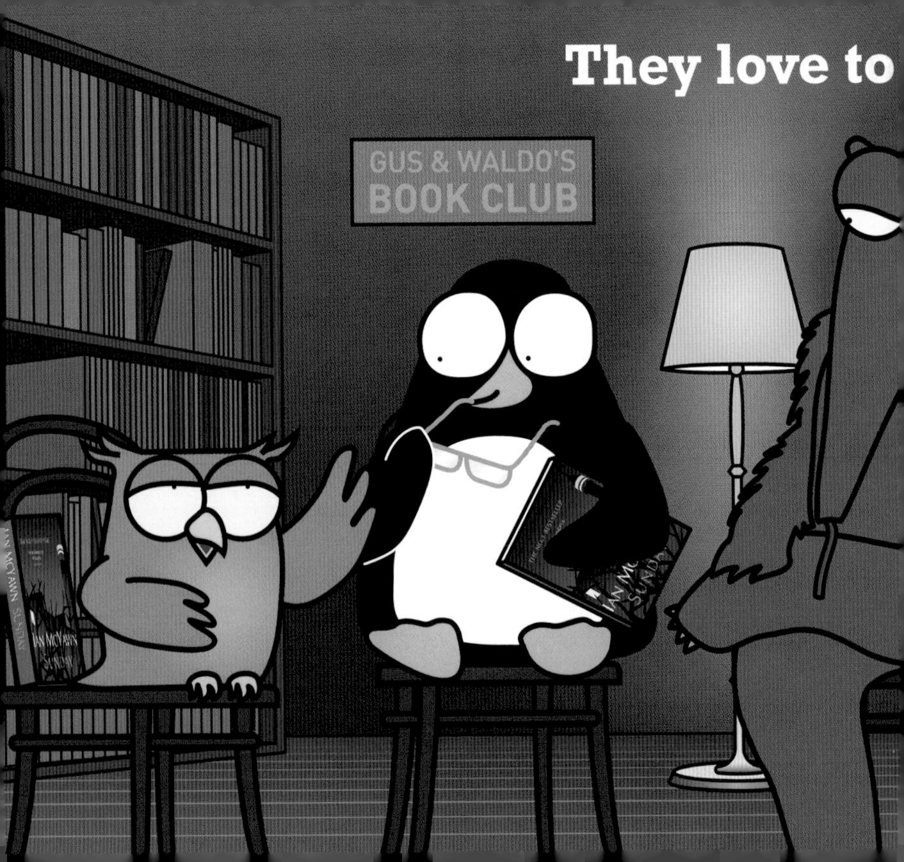
GUS & WALDO'S
BOOK CLUB
IAN MCYAWN
SUNDAY

feed their minds

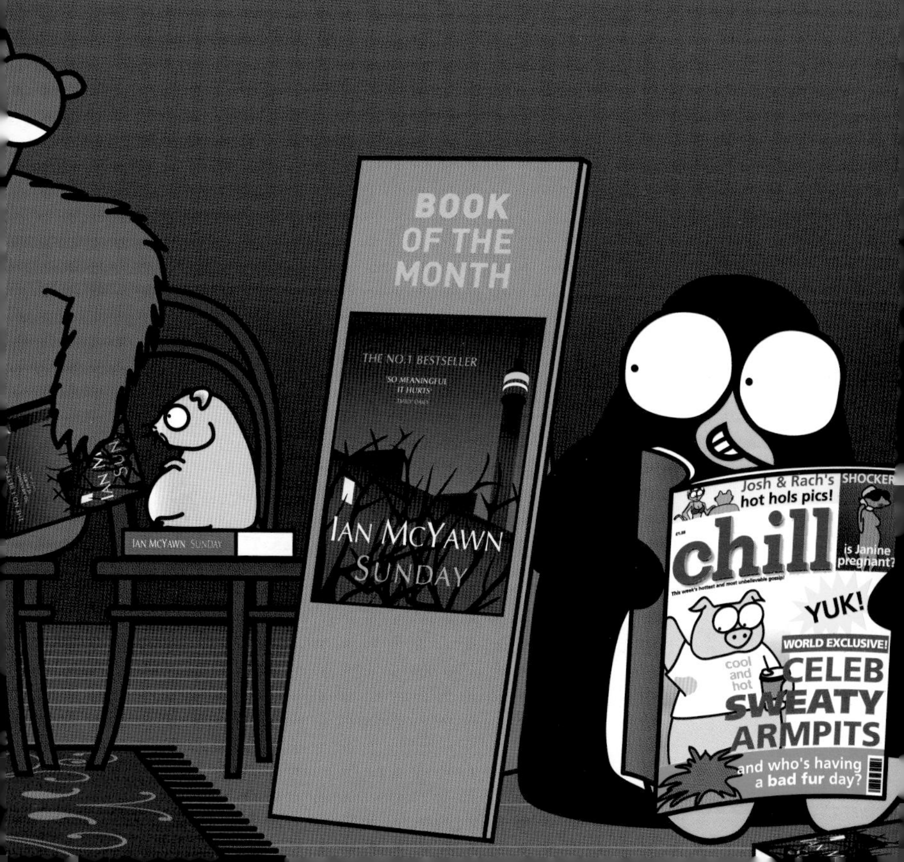
BOOK
OF THE
MONTH
THE NO.1 BESTSELLER
IAN MCYAWN
SUNDAY
IAN MCYAWN SUNDAY
Josh & Rach's
hot hols pics!
SHOCKER
chill
is Janine pregnant?
YUK!
WORLD EXCLUSIVE!
cool and hot
CELEB
SWEATY
ARMPITS
and who's having
a bad fur day?

They love to

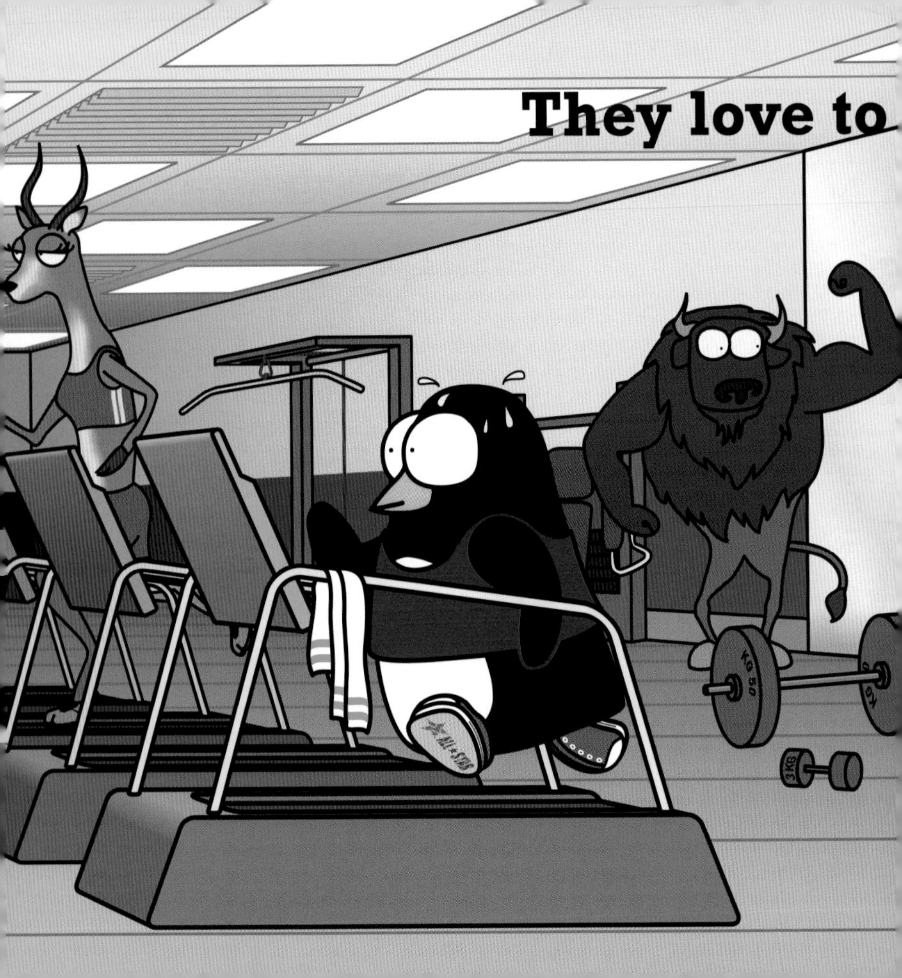
KG 50
3KG

work their bodies

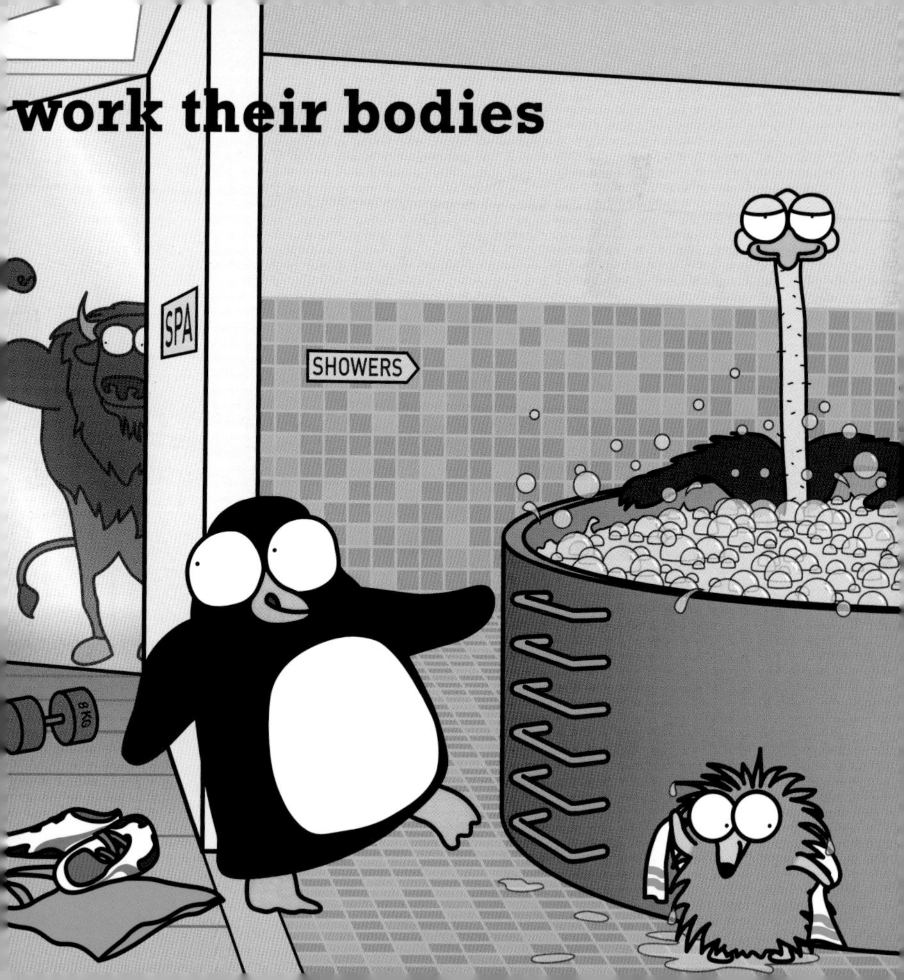
SPA
SHOWERS
8 KG

They love art...

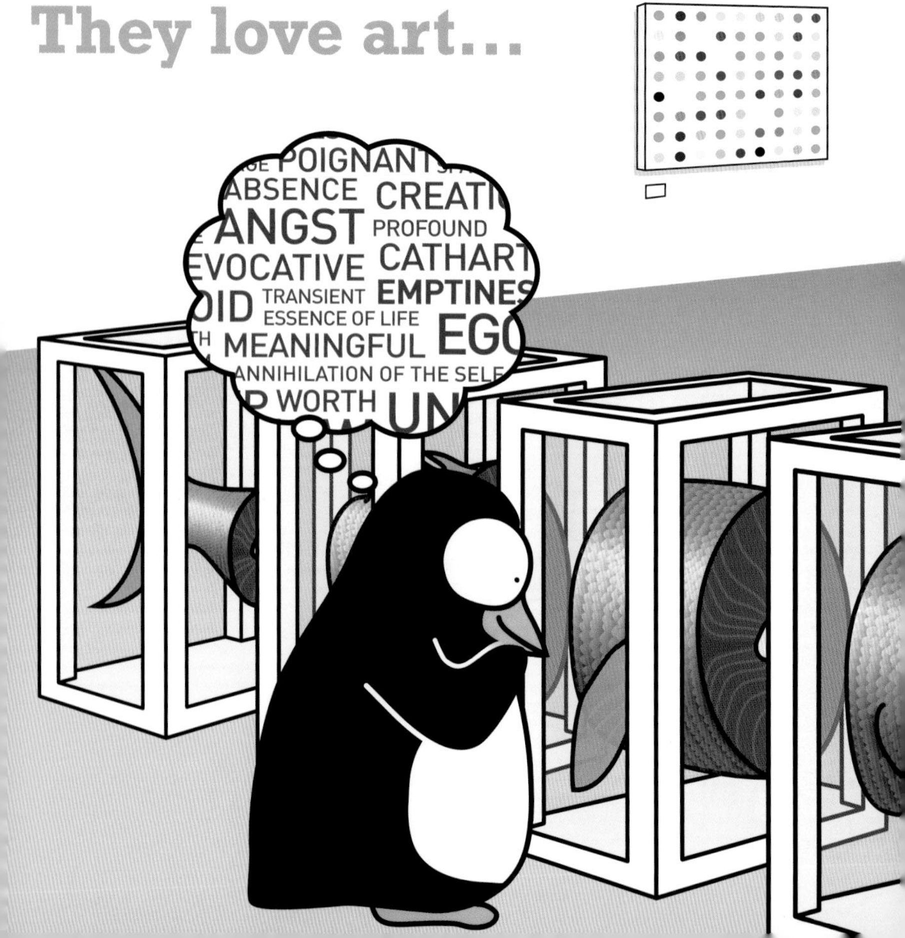
POIGNANT
ABSENCE
ANGST
PROFOUND
TRANSIENT
ESSENCE OF LIFE
MEANINGFUL
WORTH

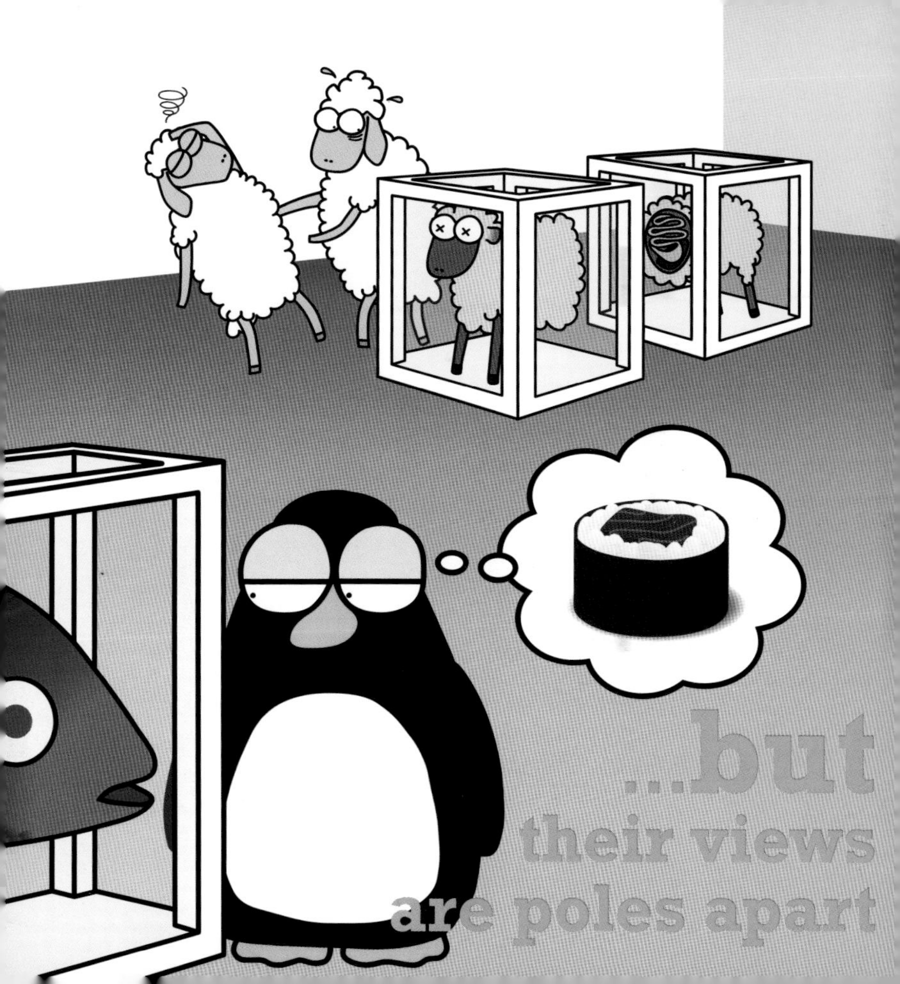
...but
their views
are poles apart

super-king-size mattress...

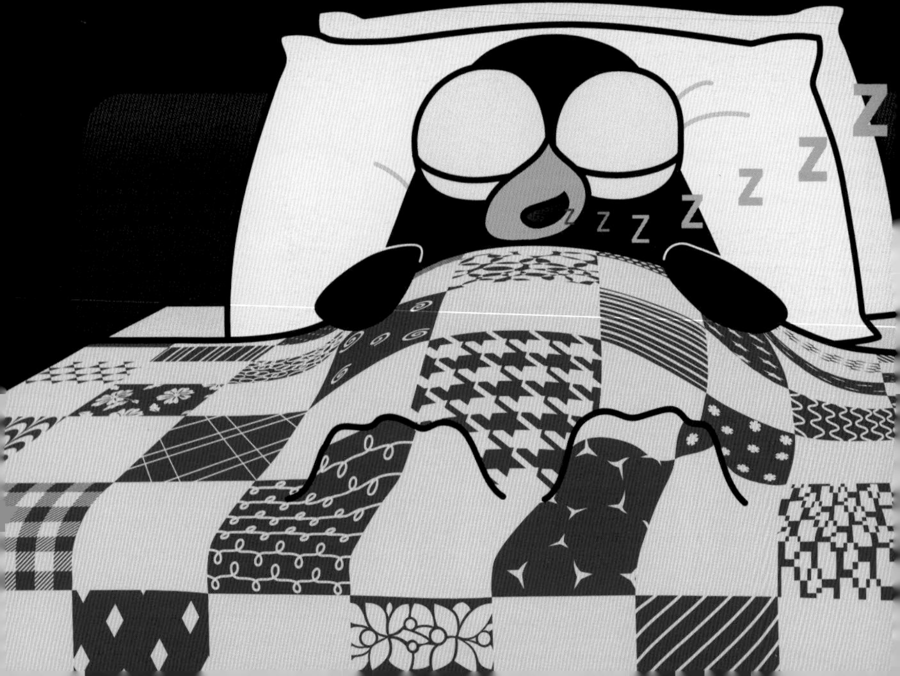

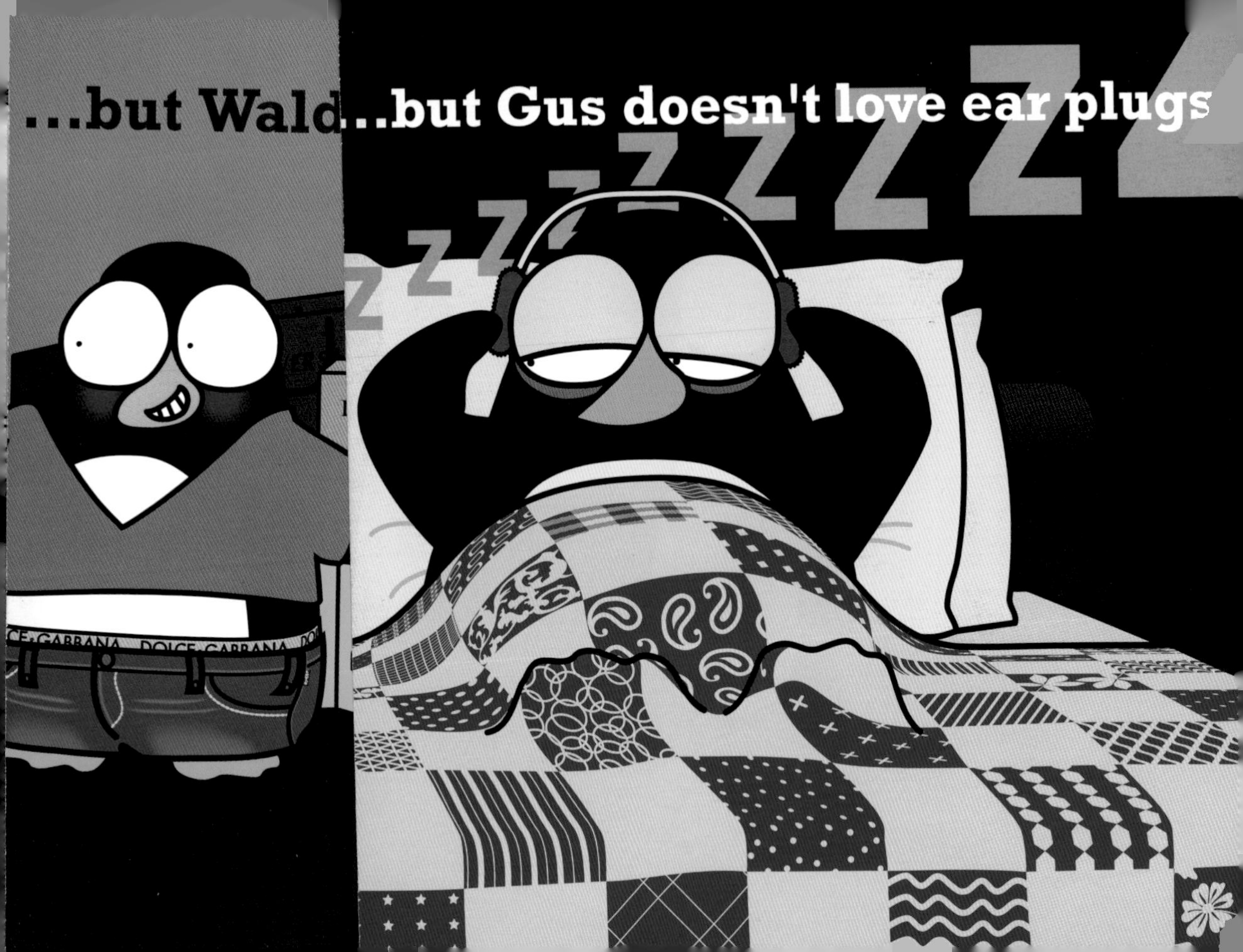
...but Wald
...but Gus doesn't love ear plugs
DOLCE GABBANA

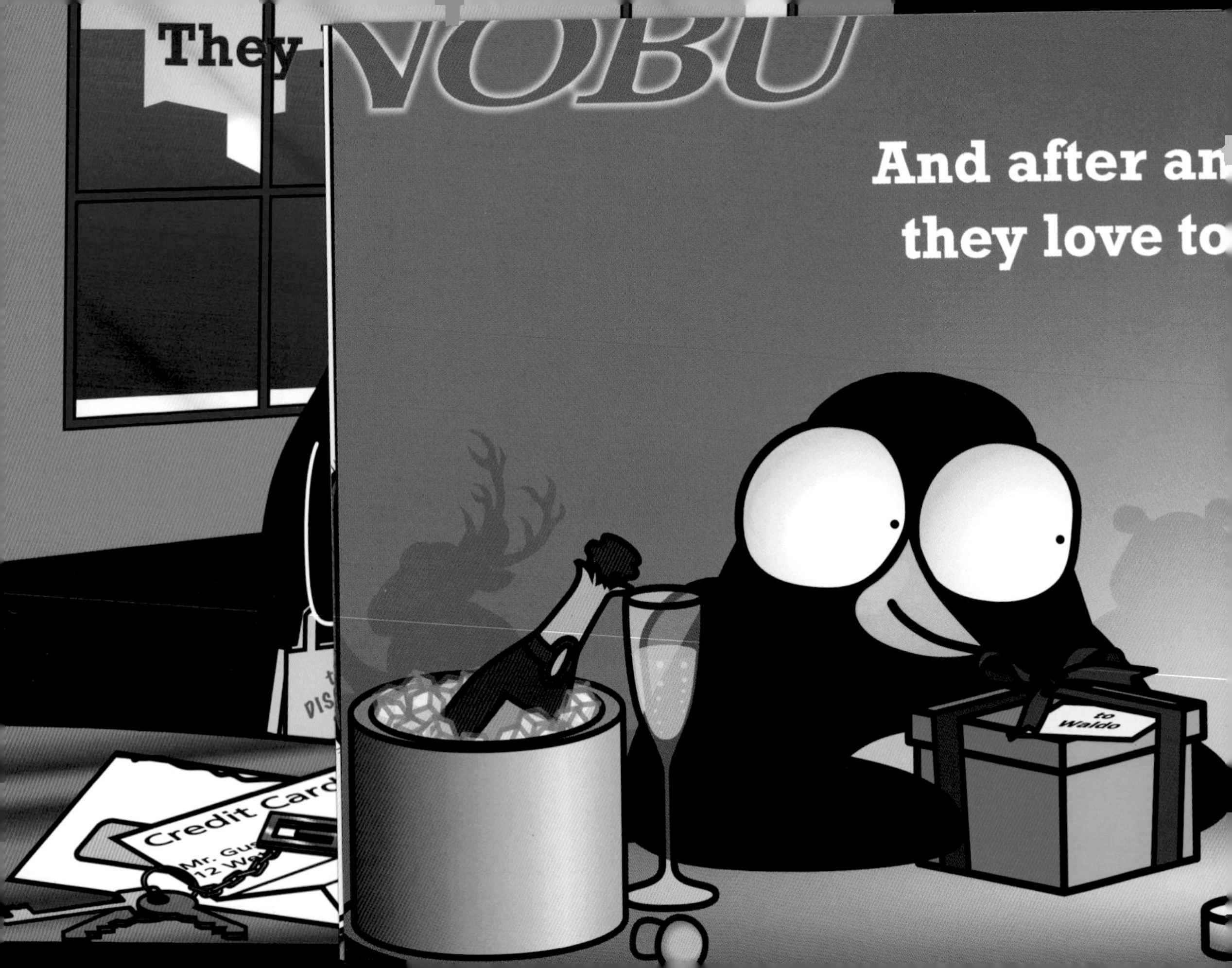
They
And after an
they love to
Credit Card
to Waldo

rgument
nake up

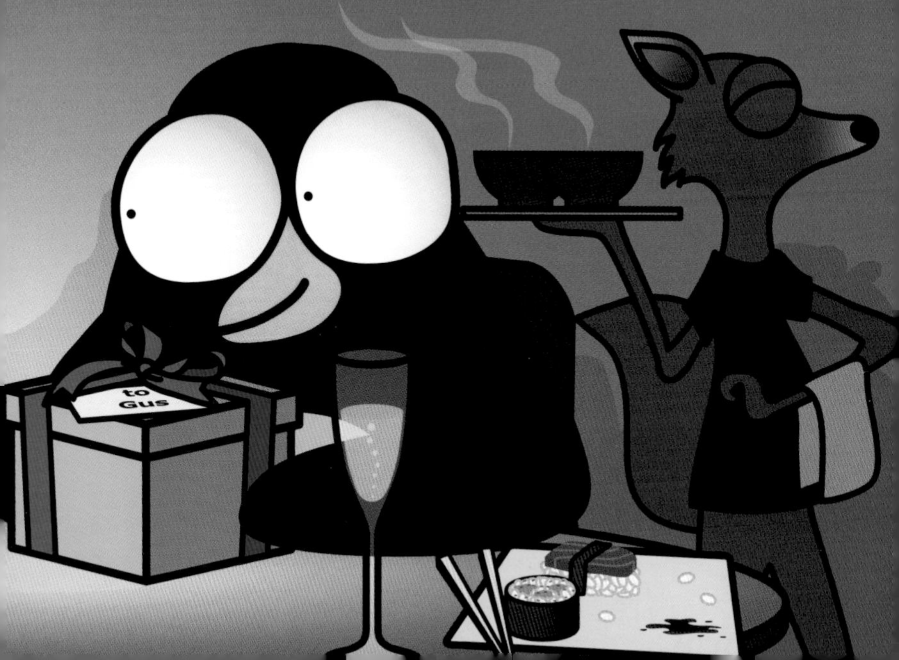
to
Gus

But sometime

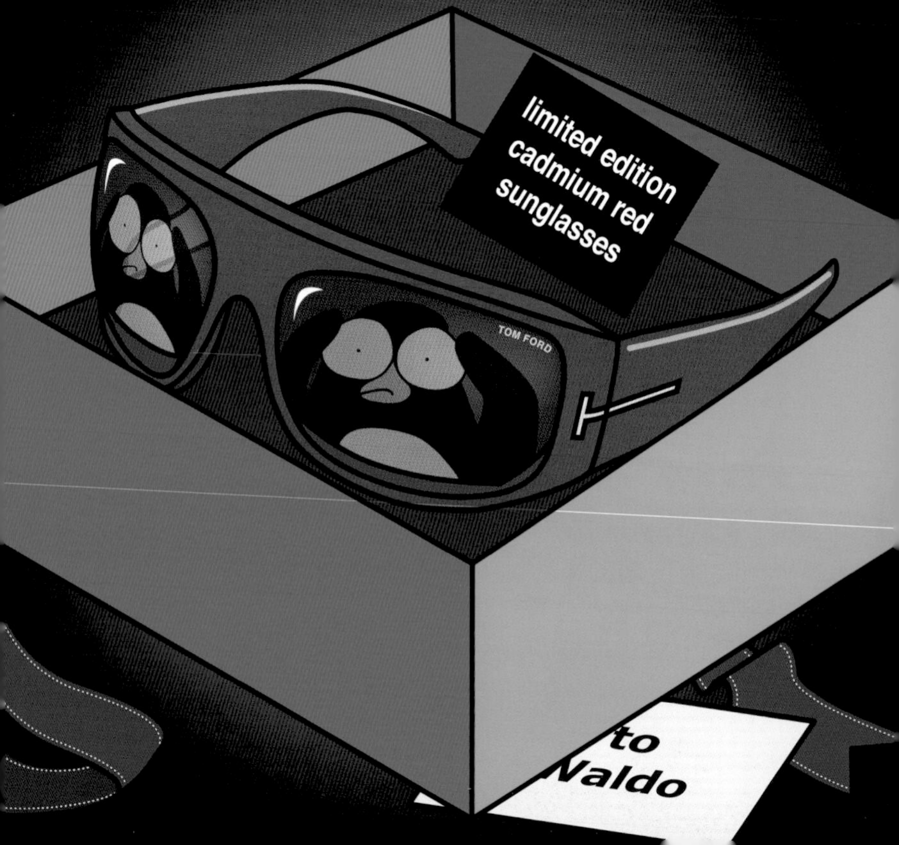
limited edition
cadmium red
sunglasses
TOM FORD
to
Valdo

hings go wrong...

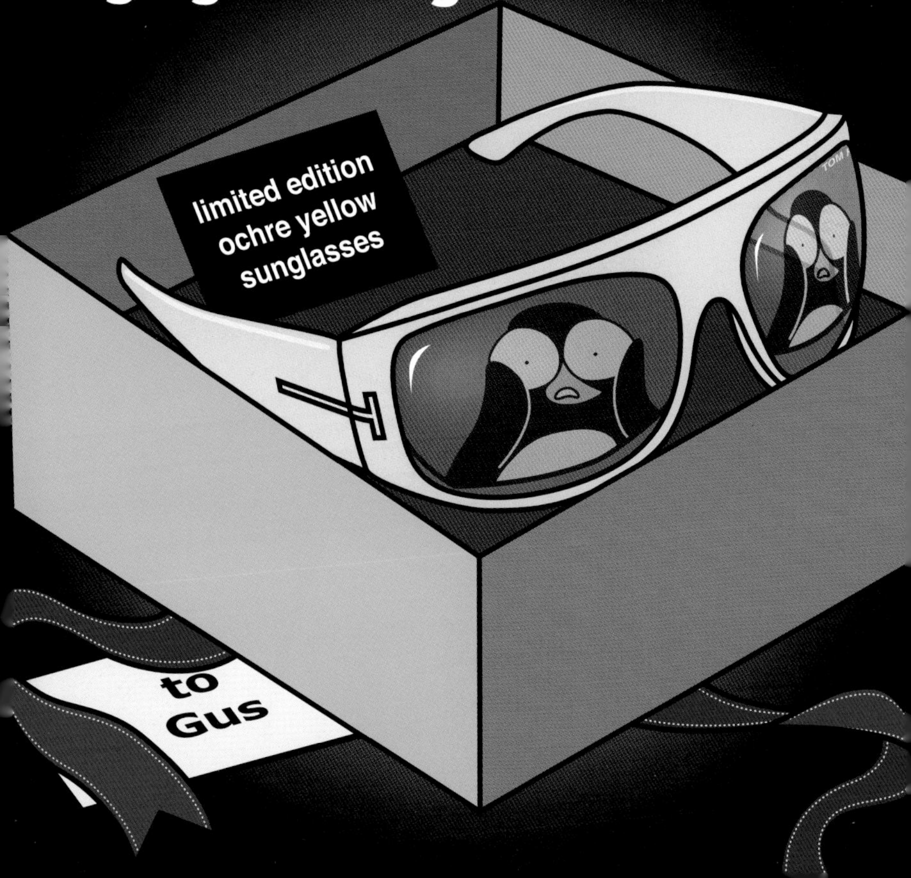
limited edition
ochre yellow
sunglasses
to
Gus

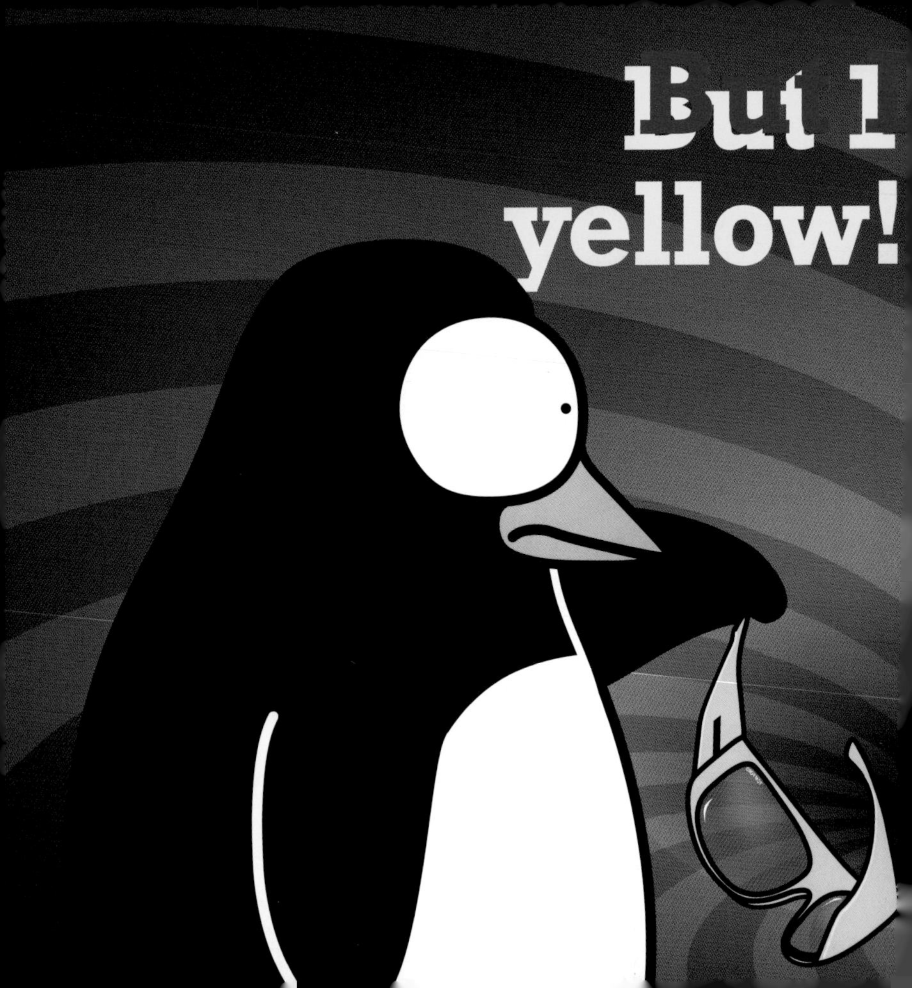
But l
yellow!

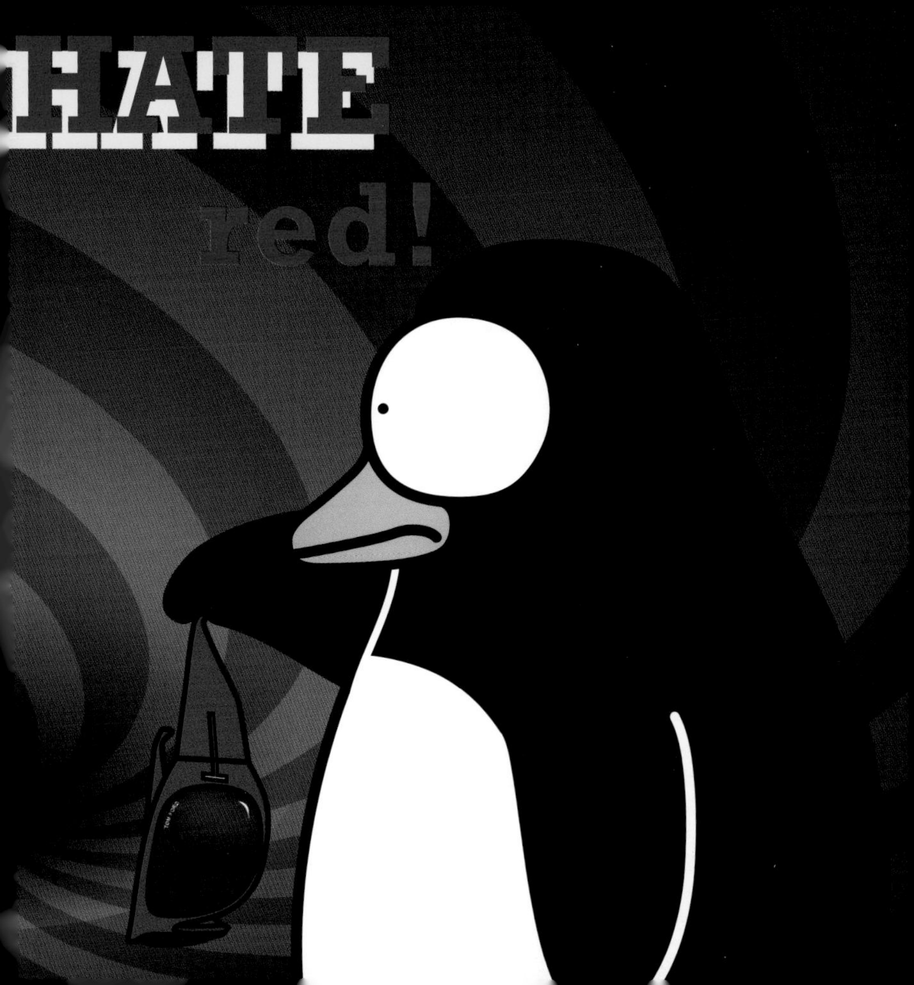
HATE
red!

OH MY

How on earth could you

What does

Do you know

Aren't we mea

Won't we be together for

Are we doo

Is this the 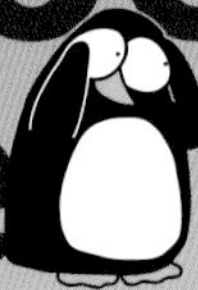 en

GOSH!

ink I'd like that colour?

his mean?

me so little?

for each other?

er till death do us part?

ed to failure?

d of our love?

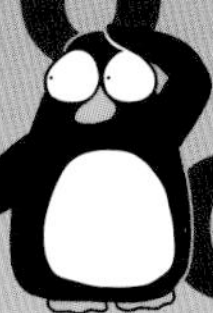

The last resort

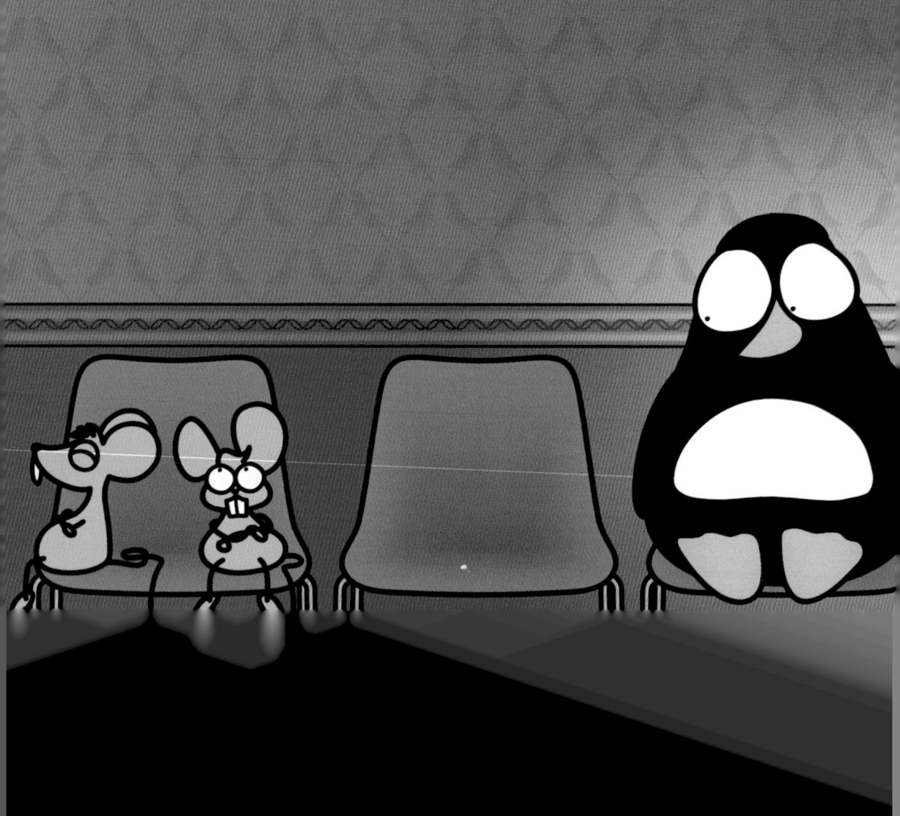

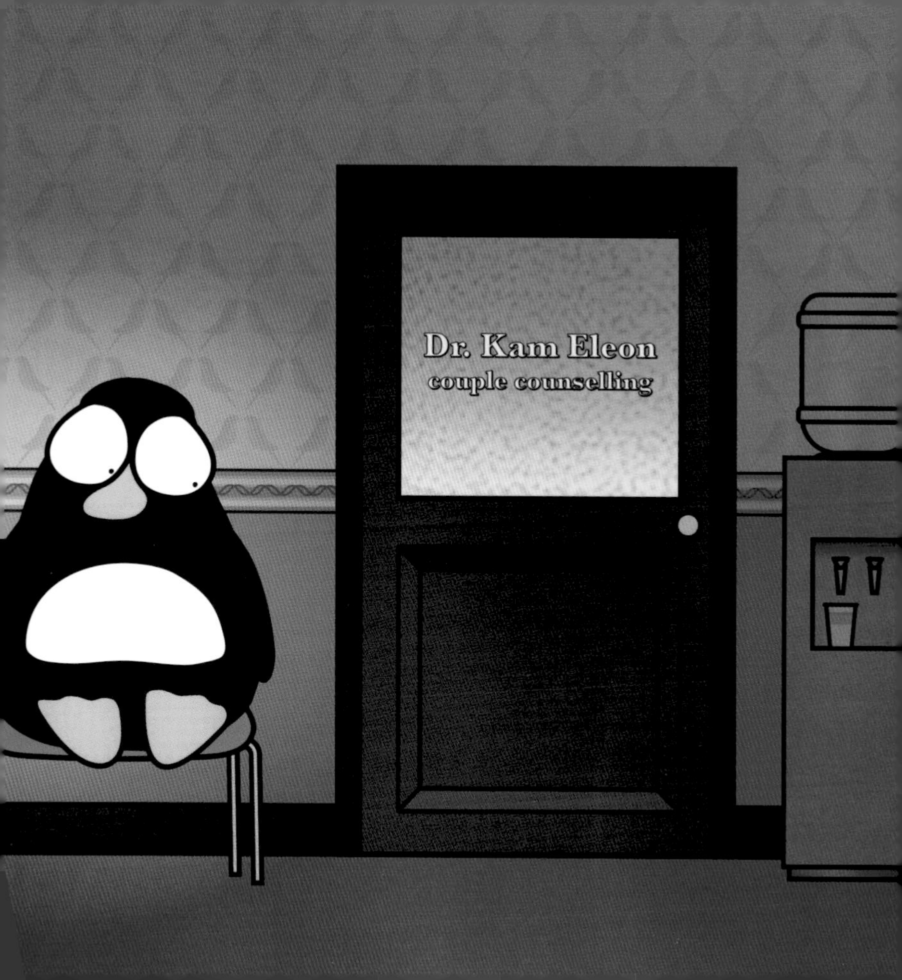
Dr. Kam Eleon
couple counselling

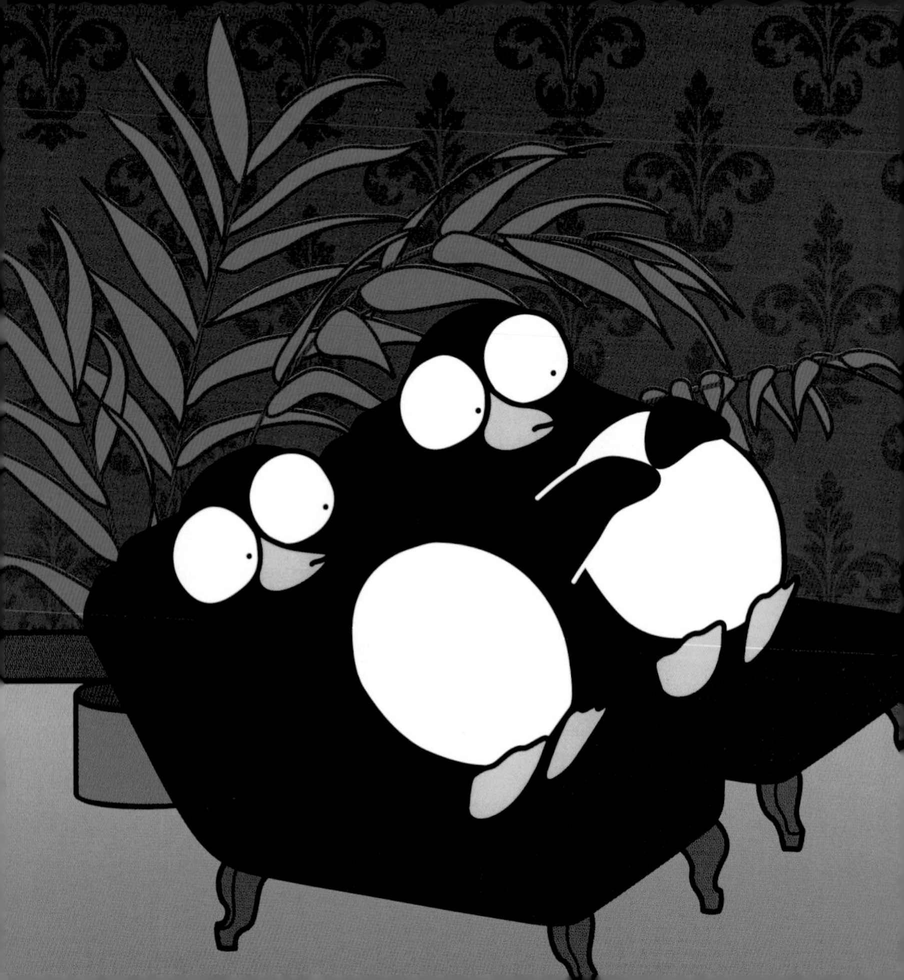

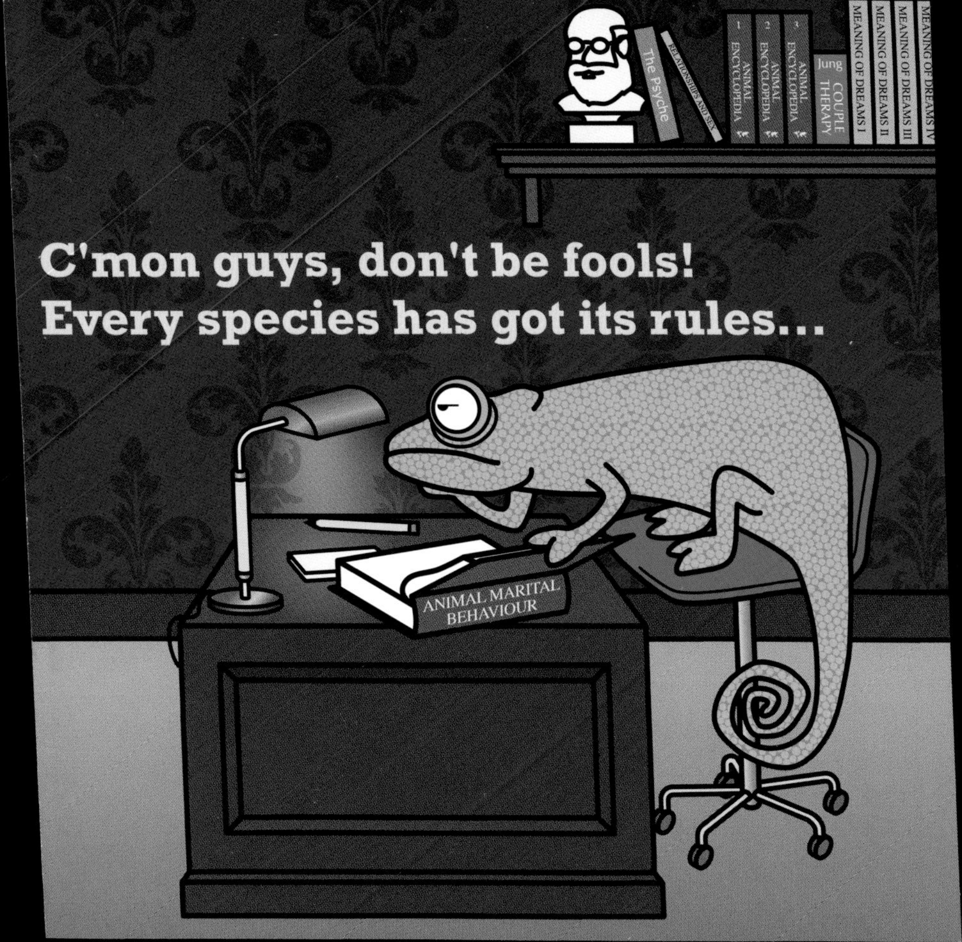
The Psyche
RELATIONSHIPS AND SEX
ANIMAL ENCYCLOPEDIA
ANIMAL ENCYCLOPEDIA
ANIMAL ENCYCLOPEDIA
Jung COUPLE THERAPY
MEANING OF DREAMS I
MEANING OF DREAMS II
MEANING OF DREAMS III
MEANING OF DREAMS IV
C'mon guys, don't be fools!
Every species has got its rules...
ANIMAL MARITAL BEHAVIOUR

them mating sea... lack of commitmen... behavioural studies carrie... pigeons have proved.

Pigeons move in a non-exclusive dat...

Penguin ('pèn-gwIn)
{Order of Spheniscɪ...
Spheniscidae, 17 sp...
Penguins are an...
birds, living pre...
...etropoli...

...enguin ...re birds, but... cannot fly. Further... 60% of their body mass is ... fat and that is no surprise... considering all the doughnuts, chocolate and pastries they scoff.

Penguins mate for life, as opposed to many other species in the animal kingdom, ... individuals often nest with th... partner at the same nes... tendency t... show a... ...f TLC their d...

...ene

...es, family

... of aquatic
...nantly in an
...habitat. Their
...nage has given
...ture's most
... often

Penguins are monogamous

...among pengu...
...jealousy ...

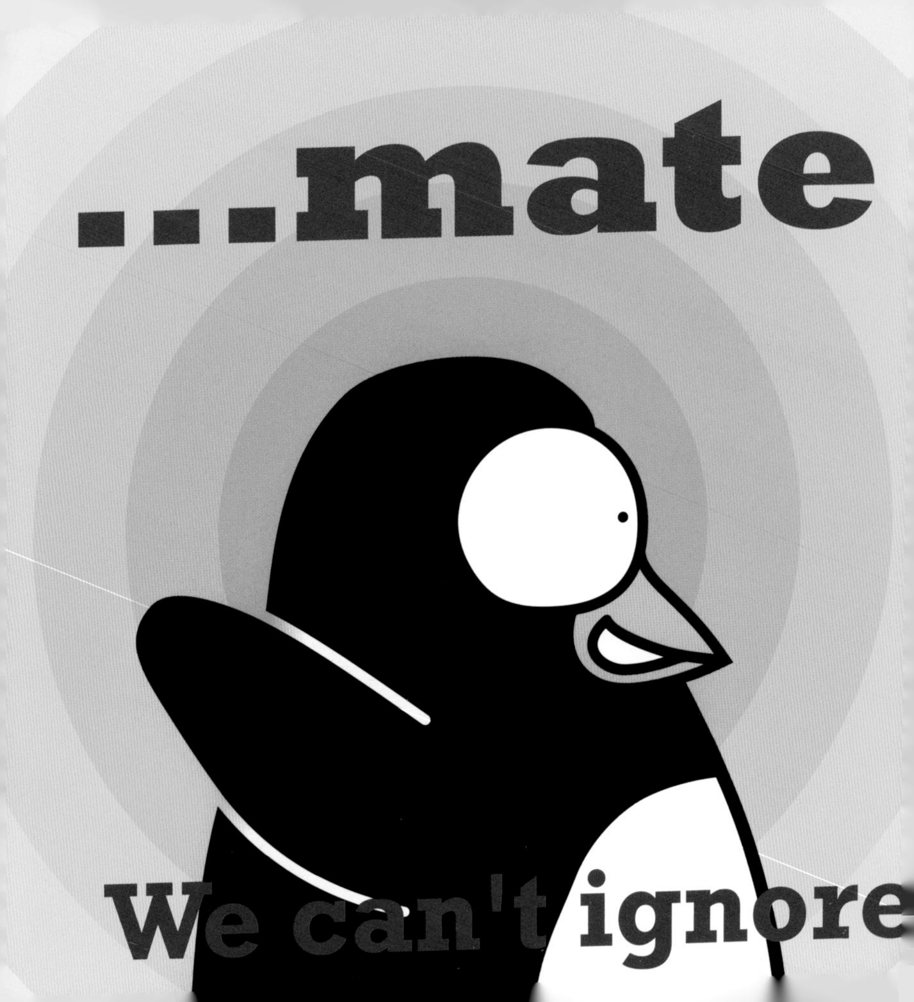
...mate
We can't ignore

for life?!

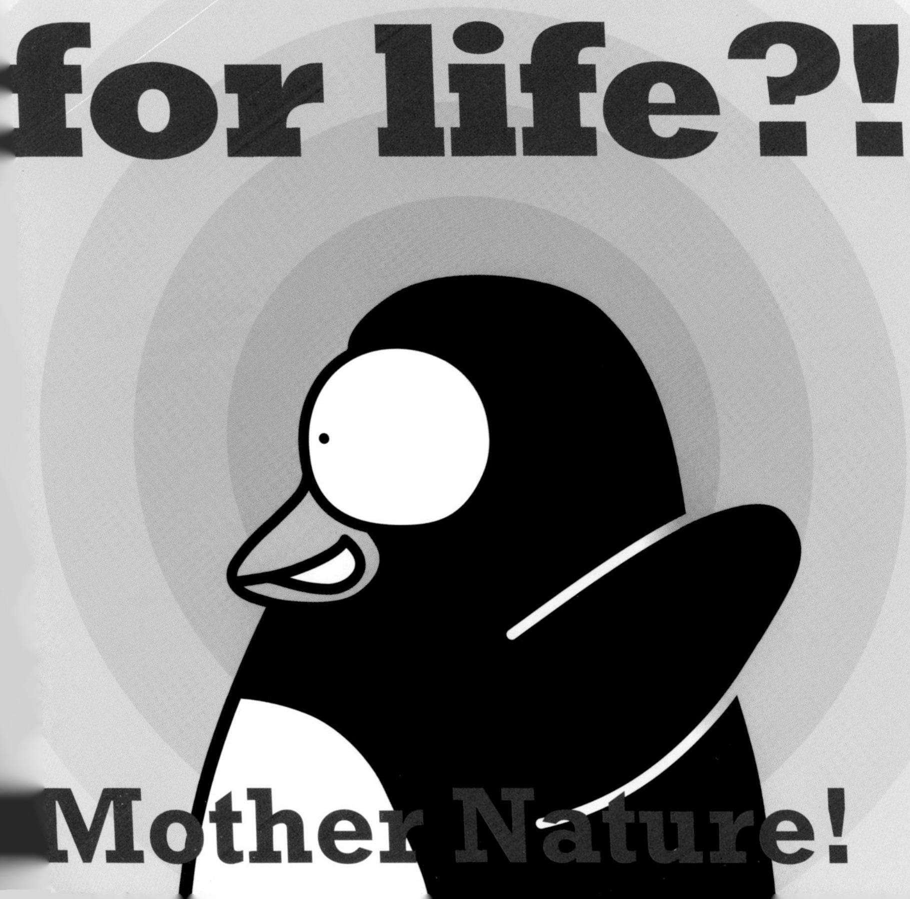

Mother Nature!

Fighting's neithe
Gus and Waldo love

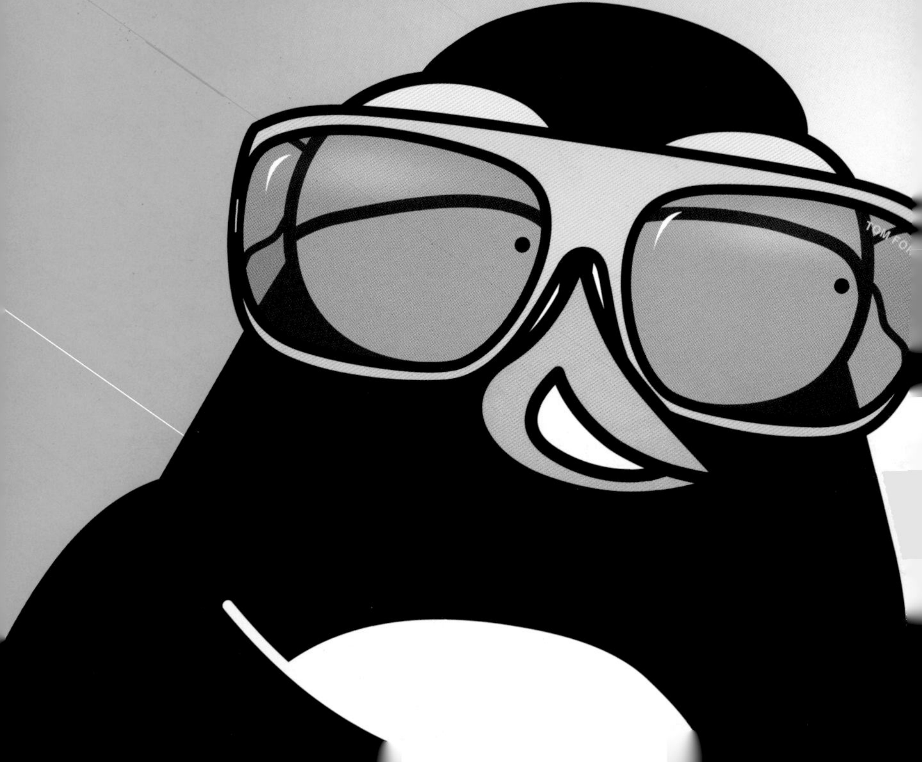

fun nor clever!

each other for ever

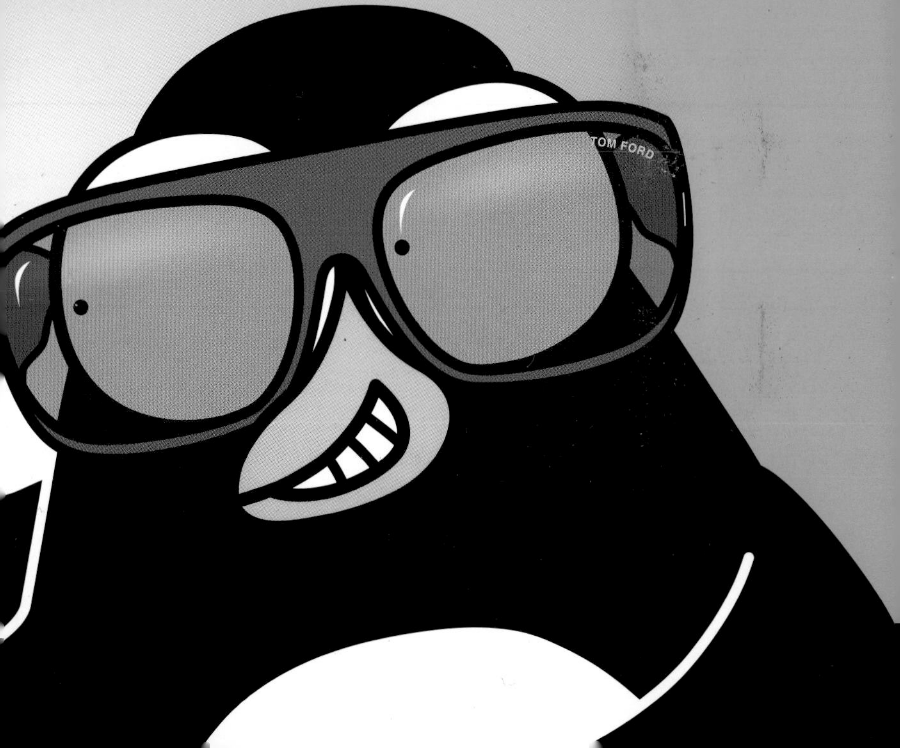
TOM FORD

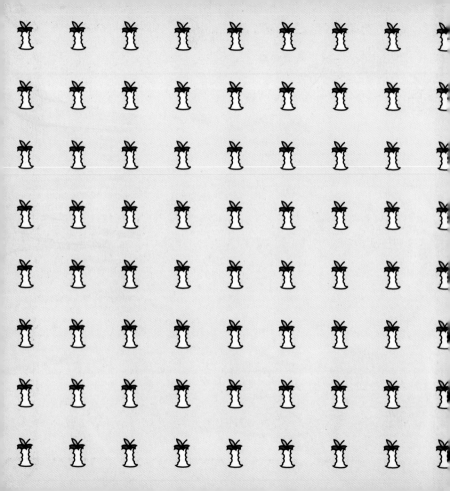